CULTURES AND COSMOS
The Cosmic Anthropological Principle

CULTURES AND COSMOS
The Cosmic Anthropological Principle

By

Baidyanath Saraswati

ARYAN BOOKS INTERNATIONAL
NEW DELHI

CULTURES AND COSMOS:
THE COSMIC ANTHROPOLOGICAL PRINCIPLE

ISBN-81-7305-258-1

Published in 2004 by
ARYAN BOOKS INTERNATIONAL
Pooja Apartments, 4B, Ansari Road, Darya Ganj, New Delhi-110 002 (India)
Tel. : 23287589, 23255799; Fax : 91-11-23270385
E-mail : aryanbooks@vsnl.com

Computer Typeset at ABI Prints & Publishing Co., New Delhi
Printed in India at B.B.N. Printers, New Delhi

Dedicated to my mother, my first teacher

Padmalata

who has completed her earthly pilgrimage

Acknowledgements

While writing this book I have lifted many ideas of several scholars. Many others in the past have spurred my thinking. I owe a special debt of gratitude to Kapila Vatsyayan who facilitated my access to the field of ontocosmological thought. The other three great people who have sharpened my awareness of many issues raised here are Raimundo Panikkar, Awadh Kishore Saran and John McKim Malville. This book is a special homage to them.

It is, indeed, a great pleasure to thank and bless my son Pratul Kumar for frequent stimulation and useful suffusions in writing these pages, and my daughter-in-law Jaya for skilfully editing the typescript. My wife Soma sustains my life while I remain engrossed in reading and writing. Without her forbearance, completing this work would not have been possible.

The dynamism, enthusiasm and understanding provided by Vikas Arya of Aryan Books International made the publication of this book possible. I wish to thank him for taking personal interest in publishing the book.

Contents

Acknowledgements *vii*
List of Illustrations *xiii*
Introduction *xv*

1. THE LIVING UNIVERSE 1
   - The Golden Germ 1
   - Brahman Zero God One 3
   - The One and the Many 6
   - God One Animal Two 7
   - Unique Forms 10
   - Animal Two Man Three 12
   - Animal Weirdness 14
   - Positive Symbiosis 15
2. THE ORDER OF NATURE 19
   - The Sacred Numbers 19
   - The Living Matter 20
   - The Fivefold Order 22
   - The Integral Vision 28
   - The Ayurvedic Tradition 28
   - The Ritualistic Tradition 31
   - The Musical Tradition 33
   - The Form and the Formless 34
   - Geometrical Forms 36
   - Conceptual Forms 37
3. THE NATURE OF SOUND 38
   - The Supreme Soundless 38
   - The Soul of Sound 39
   - The Organic Sources of Sound 40
   - The Sound of Nature 41

Sound Contexts	42
Chaotic Sound	44
Sound as Measure	45
Sound as Ritual	46
Sound and Light	47
Sound and Time	48
The Sound Beyond	49
4. THE ARENA OF SPACE	**51**
The Body of the Universe	51
The Four Quarters of the Sky	53
The Worlds of Endless Space	53
The Articulation of Sacred Space	56
Patterns in Social Space	60
Canons of Ritual Space	61
The Cosmic Play	62
Transforming Principle	67
Beyond the World of Inner and Outer	69
5. THE APPERCEPTION OF TIME	**71**
Meditation Upon Time	71
Upon Time All the Worlds Repose	72
The World Beyond Time	73
Cosmology of Time	74
Time Born with Sacrifice	75
Form of Time	77
Experiencing Time	80
Multiple Time Systems	81
Space-Time	82
Act–Order–Time	83
Transcendence of Time	85
The Presence of Future Time	86
Great Time	86
The Seven Sutras	88
6. THE ONTOLOGY OF MIND	**91**
What is Mind? Who is It?	91
What is Man? Who is He?	93
Man and Mind	94
Mind and *Maya*	94
What is Mask? Who is it?	95

Mind and Mask 96
Who Masks Whom 97
The Mind Metaphor 98

7. THE COSMIC ANTHROPOLOGICAL PRINCIPLE 101
The Manu Principle 101
One as Many 102
Man as Microcosm 103
Science as Society 104
Theodicy as Cosmodicy 105
Mind as Cosmos 107
Word as World 108
Knowledge as Experience 109
Knowledge as Culture 110
Nature as Culture 111
Ritual as Language 112
Tradition as Hiero-history 113
Unification Principle 114
Ecological Principle 116
Ordering Principle 118
Transcending Principle 119
The One Mystery 121

Bibliography *123*
Index *127*

List of Illustrations

FIGURES Page No.

1. Interlocking Elements 24
2. Interlocking Elements (Ayurvedic Tradition) 25
   5 *Elements*, 3 *Gunas*, 3 *Dosas*, 3 *Rasas*
3. Overlapping Elements 26
   Eternal (*parmanu*) Forms
   (a) *dwyanuka* (b) *trayanuka* (c) *caturnuka*
4. Overlapping Elements 27
   Gross Earth containing 50 per cent earth and in the residue portion all the remaining four elements
5. The Universe of Brahman 63
6. The Cosmic Kashi-*ksetra* 64
7. The Earthly Kashi-*ksetra* 65
8. The twelve signs of the zodiac that form the body of *Kalapurusa*, cause the division of seasons, and affect man's future, his rhythms of life, are: Mesa, Vrsa, Mithuna, Karka, Simha, Kanya, Tula, Vrschika, Dhanu, Makara, Kumbha, Mina 78

TABLE

1. The Five Elements in the Ayurveda 29
2. The Five Elements that Affect Nature 30
3. The Five Elements that Affect Man 30
4. *Yin* and *Yang* Physiology and Pathology 31
5. The Five Elements in the *Agamas* 32
6. Showing the Occurrence of *Kumbha* 67
7. The Attributes of Planets 76
8. The Vehicles of the Goddess Durga 86

Introduction

THEMES AND THESES

Semitic religions and European science have helped develop a world outlook based on *anthropic* principle. According to the first creation account in Genesis, 'So God created man in his own image, in the image of God created him; male and female created them. And God blessed them, and God said unto them: Be fruitful and multiply, and replenish the earth, and subdue it: and have dominion over the fish of the sea, and over the fowl of the air, and over every living thing that move upon the earth'. Francis Bacon, the father of modern rationalistic science, proposed that it was man's God-given right to subdue, control and exploit the natural world and every living creature. Rene Descartes converted the idea of a mathematically perfect Universe into a universal machine that ran according to mathematical laws of matter and motion. In his view, the human mind and thinking process rose above the blind machines of the natural world to stand supreme as that which defines human existence. Isaac Newton extended to this thesis further, which was seen as an innate, spiritless, atomized structure controlled by the same strictly mechanical laws. Darwinian evolution featured man with a single aspect of his particular form of intelligence, astride the ladder with all the rest of Nature beneath him.

With markers such as these, modern man places himself in the physical Universe as its master or at least as the master of the earth that he inhabits. As king of the Universe, he alone possesses the power of intelligence by which he controls the natural forces. His interplanetary travel has given him the hope and expectation that in the near future he will colonize the other parts of the Universe. Is it so?

This book is an invitation to leave behind the *anthropocentric* view of the world. Given the historical consciousness, man may have passed many mileposts but somehow he has not been able to improve his role. Modern man has developed a technocentric vision, fanning demiurgic ambitions, which stands with the destructive forces. Primordial man has a cosmocentric vision which is 'poetic-contemplative', a step forward from the 'speculative scientific' vision entertained by man today. Traditional cosmology has three crucial dimensions: the sacred Universe, the divine Order and the terrestrial existence. Modern cosmology is a special discipline and an empirical one aimed at understanding all that exists. All cultures are formed on cosmic understanding. The goal of the present enquiry is to explore the cosmic principle that makes sense for the primordial cultures.

Creationists and evolutionists today are in the midst of an ideological struggle. Christianity has challenged scientific Darwinism, arguing that evolution by Neo-Darwinian mechanism is merely a model that attempts to correlate the many diverse observations of the sciences such as physics and palaeontology. Since evolution is merely a model and not testable experimentation, one might have faith that it is true. If an alternative model for Nature correlates faith better than the evolution model, then it would be the one to believe. Therefore, evolution and creation are really competing scientific models. The main motivation in this argument is to defend a religious ideology. There is, however, a third point of view whose primary impetus is 'ontological'.

The *upanisadic* cosmology is highly complicated compared to biblical cosmogony. What it stands for is more the fruit of a vision, more an experience than mere emotions. There are two types of stable systems in the Universe of Brahman — soundless Brahman and Brahman with sound, and also two kinds of creation — creation and substitute creation. The sages had thought of Brahman (from *brh*, to expand), the 'Expanding Universe', much long before this concept was introduced in modern science. The modern theory of Big Bang is not so new. The sages had called it *bindu*, which consists of a unity of two — one static and the other dynamic. It is the dynamic aspect that expresses itself as the Universe of multiplicity. Other new paradigms such as the Milky Way galaxy, liberation of matter, galactic seeds, extraterrestrial life, the living earth, etc., can be traced back to the *upanisadic* vision. The *pauranic* cosmogony opens a broad front in ocean cosmology, in time biology, in anthropology and geology and particularly at the interface of cosmology and theology.

Quantum physics and modern psychology recognize the concept of metaphysical continuum beneath the tangible. It is said that the unseen world of intangible forces captures the flow of life. The sages had traced the 'evolution' of the living matter from the intangible to the tangible. They made no difference between matter and spirit. The elements of Nature (water, earth, air and fire), created by the cosmic forces, are ordered. Nature prohibits abrupt change in the order of the physical Universe.

The physical Universe has been characterized by the nature of sound. There are various contexts of sound. The concept of *nadabrahma* attributes consciousness to creation. Chaotic sound of the natural phenomena is associated with the cosmic reordering within the womb of the Universe. Sound is viewed as a ledger of *upanisadic* cosmology.

The sages had conceived of a world filled with matter arising out of space. Space is divided into two modes: the embodied, which is real, and the bodyless, which is *real* real. Man constructs two types of reality: mythical and mathematical. The mythical space is closely related to faith, while the mathematical space is constructed on reason. Both are the products of human consciousness, and yet opposed to each other. The mythical space merges into a physical space identified with the sacred. The sacred space echoes the cosmic play, which is boundless.

Space and time are inextricably linked. Space-time is a 'spidery thread' woven into a linear-cyclical order. In human consciousness, Act, Order and Time are inconceivable without one another. Time is not an independent reality. It is set into motion by a linear continuum of cosmic order within which changes occur in *kairological* moment and not in a chronological order.

The traditional conception of the cosmic order is not to be equated with the modern scientific laws of Nature, mathematically drawn. There are two fundamental principles — matter and life — that cause the origin of all. Matter enters into the composition of all beings. Life possesses an ontological rather than a psychological function. It is hard to separate mind from matter. Mind is a formless matter. The mind of Brahman is the universal Mind, the mind of Mind and the mother of Mind. Mind follows faith and faith follows the heart where Mind is seated. The unity of Mind and wisdom follows the divine light of the Self.

Man is conscious of Nature (matter), just as he is aware of himself. He is made of matter but he is more than matter. The Man of matter is also the Man of the Universe. His cosmic understanding (*bramhajnana*) makes him boundless because the Universe itself is boundless. At this stage of cosmic consciousness, the sages speak a language, which is called the 'inverted flute' (*ulatabansi*) or the 'twilight language' that reveals the reality symbolically. Take, for example, the spiritual symbolism of the *Mahabharata*. The genealogical descent of the of the Universe and man from spirit and matter. Shantanu (the transcendental Brahman) had two consorts: Ganga (conscious aspect of Nature as intelligence) and Satyavati (primordial Nature as matter). Ganga's son was Bhisma (universal ego) and Satyavati's children were Vyasa (consciousness of relativity and discriminating power to disarm differentiation), Chitrangada (divine primordial element) and Vichtravirya (divine ego), who had two wives: Ambika (negative doubt) and Ambalika (positive discriminating faculty). Ambika's son Dhritarashtra (the blind sense mind) had two wives: Gandhari (the power of desires) and Vaishya (the attachment of desire). Gandhari's son was Duryodhana (vainglorious desire) and his brothers, the ninety-nine other Kurus (sense tendencies). Vaishya's son was Yuyutsu (the desire to give psychological battle). Ambalika's son Pandu (*buddhi*, the pure discriminating intelligence) had also two consorts : Kunti (the power of dispassion) and Madri (the power of attachment to dispassions). Kunti had three sons: Yudhisthira (*akasa tattva,* vibratory ether element), Bhima (*vayu tattva,* vibratory air or life-force element), and Arjuna (*tejas tattva,* vibratory fire element). Madri had two sons: Nakula (*apa tattva,* vibratory water element) and Sahadeva (*kishti tattva,* vibratory earth element). Draupadi, the consort of the five Pandavas, signifies *kula kundalini*, the coiled life-force that energizes the spinal *chakras*. Sri Krisna (the universal Spirit) incarnated on earth as Kunti's brother's son.

It would seem that the Mahabharata war was hardly a historical reality. It signifies 'the spiritual and psychological battle going on between the attributes of the pure discriminative intellect in allurement with the soul and the blind sense-infatuated mind under the delusion of the ego'. This also means that cosmic metaphor can help gain certain knowledge of what is nearest and what is remotest to man. Sri Krisna as the incarnation of God Vishnu symbolizes the cosmo-theandric vision of reality.

The cosmic vision is retained in primordial cultures. Technocentric cultures cannot comprehend the unmanifested realm beneath the tangible. Every culture has a world-view that contains some 'ontology', some conception of man—what it regards as the fundamental level. Modern cultures, which 'worship' technology, strongly believe that the physical Universe can be negotiated or manipulated to ensure their cosmic future. Primordial cultures refer to a cosmological state of existence which is neither god-centric nor anthropocentric. The sages had grasped the stupendous idea of 'Expanding Universe' where God, Animal and Man originate, disappear and reoriginate endlessly. This trinity is neither a monolithic undifferentiated reality nor a pluralistic system. The ultimate constitution of the cosmos is based on the endlessly. This trinity is neither a monolithic undifferentiated reality nor a pluralistic system. The ultimate constitution of the cosmos is based on the metaphysical assumption of nothingness, that is infinity. There is a natural symbiosis between God, Animal and Man. God comes down to the world of animal and man periodically, and both animal and man return to the world of Gods. Inter-species relationship is natural. The radical relativity or *pratityasamutpada* of the Buddhist tradition explains the functioning of the cosmos. Modern man gives *anthropomorphic* meaning to the world system and develops a technocentric culture.

The interpretations of culture and cosmology may be many, but there is only one source—the *cosmic intelligence*—which extends its vitality to the entire world. Anthropocentric or technocentric understanding of the cosmos is limited. Cosmic understanding of culture is boundless. Taking the cosmic and anthropic principles together, one can discern a crucial dimension of human self-organizing system.

Throughout the text, certain ideas and concepts are repeated. This could not be avoided because there is a strong connection between the themes discussed in this book, as the reader may observe.

Chapter 1

The Living Universe

THE GOLDEN GERM

The post-Renaissance European science has now acquired a profound significance and respectability, driving all other systems of knowledge into oblivion. Computer science is the latest advance. Artificial intelligence, a specialized branch of this new science, is concerned with designing intelligent computer systems, that is, systems that exhibit the characteristics we associate with intelligent human behaviour. In other words, it is the science of making machines do things that would require intelligence. It has thrown up a mechanism through which non-computing specialists can comunicate their knowledge to the computer in their own chosen vocabulary. This is the application area called 'expert systems'. Thus, as a part of the modern system of knowledge, artificial intelligence prides itself in being *autotelic*, that is, human thought is and ought to be pursued for its own sake. This claim is consistent with the general theory of human evolution that makes man the *telos* of his own thoughts, works and deeds. Man makes himself, his own history and civilization by virture of his rational powers. He alone is the possessor of knowledge.

As against the *autotelic* science, the traditional system of knowledge gives no place of pride to human intellectual construct. For, in the beginning arose the Golden Germ (*Hiranyagarbha*), the 'womb' of the ultimate (knowledge). The rules of proofs (*pramana*) do not transcend the sacred law in the manipulation of arguments. The *Brihadaranyaka Upanisada* (3.6) presents an example of the searchings for the orgin and explanation of the world of phenomena. The question is: What is the ultimate cause of this world and how does it stand in relation to the cause? This is debated by Gargi (G) and Yajnavalkya (Y) in the following manner:

G: Since all this world is pervaded by Water, like the warp and woof in a cloth, by what indeed is Water pervaded like the warp and woof in a cloth?

Y: By Air.

G: By what indeed is Air pervaded like the warp and woof in a cloth?
Y: By the intermediate worlds.
G: By what indeed are the intermediate worlds pervaded like the warp and woof in a cloth?
Y: By the worlds of the *gandharvas*.
G: By what indeed are *gandharva*-worlds pervaded like the warp and woof in a cloth?
Y: By the worlds of the Sun.
G: By what indeed are the worlds of the Sun pervaded like the warp and woof in a cloth?
Y: By the worlds of the Moon.
G: By what indeed are the worlds of the Moon pervaded like the warp and woof in a cloth?
Y: By the worlds of the Stars.
G: By what indeed are the worlds of the Stars pervaded like the warp and woof in a cloth?
Y: By the worlds of the Gods.
G: By what indeed are the worlds of the Gods pervaded like the warp and woof in a cloth?
Y: By the worlds of Indra.
G: By what indeed are the worlds of Indra pervaded like the warp and woof in a cloth?
Y: By the worlds of Prajapati.
G: By what indeed are the worlds of Prajapati pervaded like the warp and woof in a cloth?
Y: By the worlds of Brahma.
G: By what indeed are the Brahma's worlds pervaded like the warp and woof in a cloth?
Y: O Gargi, do not question too much. Let not your head fall off. O Gargi, you are questioning too much about a divinity which is not to be questioned. O Gargi, do not over-question.

Thereupon Gargi retired.

In this argumentation, following the logic what every effect should have a cause, Gargi starts with Earth which has Water as its cause, for in the order of creation the Element Earth is shown as having come out of Water Element. Water, which is the cause, pervades the Earth, its effect. Now, this Water in its turn is only an effect and its cause is shown to be Air, which is subtler than Water. Again Air as the effect, Ether or the intermediate world becomes the cause. Tracing the causes further to more and more subtle principles, Yajnavalkya goes on enumerating the chain of causes and effects, indicating that causes are subtler than their respective effects. In the *upanisadic* vision, everything here is one Cosmic Being called Brahman. What is the cause of the worlds of Brahman, was Gargi's last question. This question is not answered by Yajnavalkya on the ground that the question of question (*atiprasna*) is inadmissible in logic. Reasoning cannot furnish an answer to this question. Intellect can know the causes and effects and not the cause of all causes. Yajnavalkya wants that one should not depend upon logical reasoning to transcend *Hiranyagarbha*, the self-disclosure of the ultimate mystery itself. The Vedic hymn presents a profound insight into unfolding of the reality

> In the beginning arose the Golden Germ:
> he was, as soon as born, the Lord of Being,
> sustainer of the Earth and of this Heaven.
>
> —*Rigveda* X, 121

The Golden Germ disclosed itself. The idea behind the symbolism of the golden (light) germ (divine life) is that there is a self-existing process within the eternal 'womb' of the reality (the Cosmic Intelligence) and a production (life).

BRAHMAN ZERO GOD ONE

What remains the keystone of our edifice, spiritual knowledge, is a set of questions and answers pertaining to the Universe:

> Where did the Universe come from?
> The Universe came from Brahman.
> What is Brahman?
> Brahman is the universal Self.
> Is Brahman the creator of the Universe?
> No, Brahman itself is the Universe.
> How did the Universe start off?

The Universe did not start off at any particular time. It is set in eternal cycles of creation, existence and dissolution.

How can the Universe change and yet remain eternal?

Although space and time have a beginning and an end, both continue forever through a self-organizing system that repeats itself endlessly.

Is the Universe a machine called Brahman?

Not, indeed, in the Newtonian sense of a deterministic machine.

What, then, is the Hindu concept of the Universe? To what extent does it relate itself to other traditions?

The Hindu perception of the Universe is different from that of the Semitic tradition. But it does not seem to be at much variance with the theories of modern science.

The Universe at large has an ontological independence of its own. It is characterized by the term Brahman, from the root *brh*, to expand. Surprisingly and yet not so surprisingly, the ancient sages had thought of an 'expanding Brahman' long before the concept of 'Expanding Universe' was introduced in modern science. Then came along the notion of *nada* or *shabda* Brahma, which refers to the Cosmic Sound, the turning of the world.

Most cosmologists today believe that Big Bang was the abrupt creation of the Universe from literally nothing: no space, no time, no matter. The ancient sages had said so in exactly the same language:

At first there was neither Being nor Non-being.
There was no air, nor yet sky beyond.
There was no death, nor yet deathlessness;
Of night or day there was not any sign.

—*Rigveda* X, 129

In that state of absolute vacuity, Brahman breathed without breath by its own impulse.

Further, scientists have suggested that at the time of 'Big Bang', the Universe was infinitesimal and infinitely dense. It is fitting that the *upanisadic* sages had called it *bindu*, the dimensionless point, literally a drop. It comprises the unity of two— one static and the other dynamic. It is the dynamic aspect that expresses itself as the Universe of multiplicity but it essentially remains one—the epitome of all. In geometry, the point (*bindu*) is the Sun, that is, a centre with a circumference. There is a centre and a periphery, diameters and radii. The circle is a point expanded. The meeting of two equal lines forms a square and three lines come together to form a triangle. These primary forms are fundamental to Hindu thought.

The concept of zero *(sunya)* Brahman denotes the notational as well as the void or the absence of the notational place. On the mathematical function of zero it has been said that numbers, both positive and negative, undergo no change when zero is added to or subtracted from them. But when subtracted from zero, a positive number becomes negative and a negative number positive.

A number, when multiplied by zero, becomes zero; and when divided by zero it becomes *khahara*.

The *khahara* is an infinite quantity. Its nature is elucidated by a significant analogy of Brahman. In this numerical quantity called *khahara*, there will be no change, whether or not much is added to it or subtracted from it, just as no change takes place in the infinite and immutable godhead, though numerous beings are absorbed in it at the time of destruction of the world or numerous beings issue forth from it at the time of the creation of the world.

Generally, the concept of zero when applied to Brahman, the absolute, is unthinkable in itself. Metaphysically, it is identified with both fullness and emptiness. Fullness is the non-dual infinity of Brahman. The Universe that is unborn and that which is born is full.

> That is Fullness, this is Fullness,
> From Fullness comes Fullness.
> When Fullness is taken from Fullness
> Fullness yet remains.
>
> —*Brihadaranyka Upanisada* 5.1

The opposite of fullness is emptiness. Brahman (gram. neuter) is described as lacking positive attributes: It is neither gross nor subtle, neither short nor long and neither wind nor space. It is unattached without taste or smell, without eyes or ears, without speech or mind, without head, without breath, without face, without any measure and without inside or outside. It neither eats nor is it eaten.

The description of Brahman as full and empty, shows that it is beyond dialectical opposition between time and timelessness, formed and unformed, mortal and immortal, actual and beyond and so on.

The philosophy of *sunya* Brahman as a coherent reality, may help understand the scientific theory that the Universe had been borrowed from the vacuum. In quantum physics something can come out of nothing for a while but eventually the debt has to be paid. The manner of demise of the Universe as a whole is determined by the nature of its birth. Amazingly, the sages have defined Brahman precisely in the same language:

> That from which beings are born,
> that by which, once born, they live,
> that into which, once dead, they enter.

Cosmologists are of the opinion that about 100 billion stars, including the Sun, make up the Milky Way galaxy, a wheel-shaped structure. The galaxy is itself a part of a group of galaxies that form a cluster, while the clusters in turn form the supercluster of many thousands of galaxies. Powerful telescopes reveal that this pattern of hierachical clustering prevails throughout the cosmos. What binds the Universe together are the cosmic strings which are hypothesized to have some bizarre properties. Long long ago, sage Yajnavalkya had said this to his disciple Aruni: This world and next world and all beings and all natural phenomena are strung together by the thread, the Inner Controller, the Immortal, the Brahman.

THE ONE AND THE MANY

Recently, a maverick British scientist, Jim Lovelock, has proposed the *Gaia* hypothesis, which has stirred a fierce debate among biologists and ecologists but it fits naturally into the new paradigm of self-organizational complexity. *Gai* is the name of Greek Goddess of Earth and it points out that the various forms of life on Earth are components of one living organism. *Hiranyagarbha* is a cosmic metaphor attributed to the origin of the Universe. Here gold symbolizes the principle of light shining forth from within the womb of darkness. The sap within the Egg originally existed in an undifferentiated form but later were born the seven primeval ancestors or types of seven differentiated life forces (Mind, Life and the Five Elements of matter). The Egg floated on water for thousand years and then something triggered it off. It split into two halves and the whole Universe came out into existence. This auto-fission of the 'One into two and two into many' is fundamental to ancient Indian thought.

The organic units of the Universe are further clarified by an anthropic metaphor. From the limbs of *Purusa*, the Cosmic Person, everything originated: Strophes and Melodies, Horses and Other Animals, the Four Castes of Men, the Sky, the Atmosphere, the Ocean, the Earth, the Moon, the Sun, the Fire, the Wind and the King of Gods.

The idea of organic relationship is pursued to a high degree of sophistication:

> The Self is the honey of all beings
> and all beings are honey for the Self.
> As the one Wind, once entered into a house,
> Takes on the forms of all that is in it,
> So the One inmost Self of every being
> Takes on their several forms,
> (remaining) without (the while).
>
> —*Brihadaranyaka Upanisada* 2.5

Two things have come out clearly from the *upanisadic* passages. First: One is not the all, that is, One is not the sum total; One is subsistent in Many. Second: Although the world of plurality has emerged out of the One (Self), the One is not affected by the defects of the Many.

The relationship between the unmanifest (Brahman) and the manifest (Universe) is formed by a divine entity called God. As an aspect of Brahman, God is transcendent and as an architect of the Universe it is immanent. Brahman is without a name, without a form and without a function. God is with names, with forms and with functions. As an innermost aspect of Brahman, God's uniqueness lies in its concurrent existence in all forms. God operates within the self-organized Universe of Brahman and hence has no absolute freedom. But within its own sphere, it exercises its instinct powers and so are named the God of creatures (Brahma), the God of sustaining force (Vishnu) and the God of dissolution and death (Mahesha). There are many Gods with many names, with many forms. They are so much a part of the forms and functions of the observable Universe that with the extinction of the Universe they all dissolve in the same manner and at the same moment, as other beings and things of the Universe die.

The mathematics of Brahman is: a - a = o; a + o = a; a - o = a; a x o = o; a/o becomes infinity. The geometry of God as *bindu* breaks into plurality of primary forms: the square, the circle and the triangle.

GOD ONE ANIMAL TWO

The theory of Big Bang implies the appearance not merely of matter and energy but of space and time as well. In other words, the physical Universe was created with time. Christian and Muslim theologians have also said that God created the Universe with time. The Hindu perception of time and creation is far more complex.

The cosmic sound is an aspect of Brahman which is beyond cause and effect, beyond time and space and beyond creation. But within the timeless-spaceless Universe of Brahman, God is born with time to create a physical Universe (space) in time. With the death of God, the physical Universe also dies out and a new cycle of creation and dissolution begins. And thus it goes on endlessly.

As the tradition has it, the smallest unit of the cosmological time is *yuga*, a creation age. The four *yugas* make up a *mahayuga* of 12,000 years. One day of Brahma, the creator of physical Universe, constitutes thousand fourfold *yugas* and during the life of Brahma, fourteen Indra (the King of Gods) fall from Heaven and die. This is a Brahma age. The ages of two Brahmas constitute the age of one Vishnu, the sustainer of the Universe. At the end of the age, Vishnu also perishes. The age of Mahesha, the destroyer, is double the age of Vishnu. Mahesha also perishes at the end of his age. When everything perishes there comes the deluge (the great flood). After that, for one-hundred-and-twenty Brahma years, the Universe remains a desolate void. In that deep eternal silence Vishnu sleeps on a banyan leaf on the surface of water. That is the beginning of the next great age. From Vishnu's navel, a lotus-stalk grows up and on the top of the stalk in the lotus flower, Brahma comes into being. Brahma does penance before Vishnu and extols him. The great Vishnu confers on Brahma the power of creation of the subjects. That Brahma perishes along with the deluge and in his place another Brahma is born. Thus, in the lifetime of Vishnu, two Brahmas come into being and perish.

There is no mono-creation, no linear time. The creations performed by Brahma are of two kinds: *sarga* (creation) and *pratisarga* (substitute creation). In the first *kalpa* (a thousand *mahayugas*) when a Brahma is born from the lotus, certain creations are made. The things thus originated, do not undergo destruction in the evening or at the end of the *kalpa*. They are *sarga*. On that day and everyday of the life of Brahma, they help Brahma in his work of creation. In a sense they are Prajapatis (the lords of emanation). A Brahma creates in his first morning not only persons having a long life as he himself has but also creations which have a history only up to the end of that day such as *lokas* (worlds), minerals, plants, animals, humanity, etc. Creation is called *prakriti sristi* (natural creation) and substitute creation is *aprakriti sristi* (unnatural creation). At the end of *kalpa*, fire and rain, which destroy the Universe, occur and all the unnatural creations are destroyed. In all the mornings, following the first morning of a Brahma, substitute creation takes place and they are destroyed at the end of each *kalpa* by fire and rain.

God takes three kinds of incarnations—that which has full power is *avatara*; that which has power only for the time being is *avesa*; and that which has only partial incarnation is *amasavatara*. The incarnations of Vishnu are countless. The hermits, Manus and Devas and sons of Manus are Vishnu's incarnations in part. Complete incarnations are ten in number. Of the ten, the first three are animal forms (Fish, Turtle and Boar), the fourth is a composite form (Lion-Man), fifth is a dwarf and the next four are fully developed humans. The tenth incarnation is yet to come.

It is said, when injustice and lawlessness abound in the Universe, Vishnu will incarnate in the world in various forms and shapes and will drive away injustice and will reinstate righteousness. The basis and the indeclinable semen virile of all the incarnations is this spirit of the Universe. The order of ten *avatars* is significant insofar as it is complete incarnations and it begins with the animals associated with the early phase of creation. This gives animal a position in the order of reality only next to God. The following description and symbolization will clarify the point.

Fish (*Matsya*)

Once a demon stole the Vedas from the side of Brahma and with them he went under water to the bottom of the ocean and hid himself there. So, Vishnu took the form of a fish to retrieve the stolen Vedas. The meaning is clear: The fish is an appropriate symbol of the Cosmic Egg. Fish live under a great variety of conditions—at the surface of sea, in mid-water, at the bottom or buried in the sand or mud. Their greatest quality is found in their capacity to produce eggs. The resemblance between the developing child in the womb called the foetus and the fish in water symbolizes the primeval mother-principle. The recovering of the hidden Vedas (knowledge) by the fish refers to the principle of simultaneity of life and knowledge. The finding of palaeontologists also gives a sense to this vision of Cosmic Fish. The first vertebrates are known from scrappy fossils of bony plates from the late Cambrian. These are ascribed to agnathan (literally 'jawless') fish which flourished in fresh water and marine environments in the Silurian and Devonian period as generally heavily armoured forms. They declined thereafter and are represented today by the eel-like lampreys and hagfish. Among Hindus of eastern India today, the lamprey variety is a taboo even for those who are fish-eaters.

Turtle (*Kurma*)

In their venture to procure ambrosia from the sea of milk, the gods and the demons used the Mount Mandar as churn-drill and the huge snake Vasuki as churning rope. As the process began, the churn-drill, having no fixation at the bottom, sank. Vishnu then took the form of a turtle, got under the Mandar mountain and lifted it up on his back. Here the turtle, appearing in the cosmic creation of Earth, symbolizes the spatial expansion. Its association with the celestial honey and the churning of the milky ocean means emergence of life-sap (*prana*). Turtle is the symbol par excellence of life and the principle of contraction and expansion which follows in the emergence of the creature. As an aquatic animal, it represents a stage in cosmic creation when the Earth emerges from the primeval waters.

Boar (*Varaha*)

Once a demon got down into the primeval ocean and began to beat the waves with his cudgel. The ocean started to sway and surge. The God of Water was terrified. He approached Vishnu for help. Vishnu took the form of a boar and came to the ocean. The demon took the Earth in his hand and ran into nether world. The boar followed and killed him. Thus the Earth was recovered. The imagery of the boar lifting the Earth from the depths of the ocean speaks of the dynamic principle of creation. When Earth was redeemed from the dark depths of the primeval state of dissolution and darkness, the creative process of Light or Life became effective. The boar is an animal in which thick layers of fat underlie the skin. It also lives in mud. The real meaning is that the cosmos was created by Surya (Sun), the fat-dripping animal. The dripping fat is the temperature of its rays, the heat radiated by the Sun throughout the space. This is true not only with the Sun around which the Earth revolves but to millions or billions of other Suns in the space, all of which are dripping this symbolic fat from which creation in different forms is taking place.

Lion-man (*Narasimha*)

A ferocious demon became arrogant due to his power and became oppressive. Vishnu assumed a composite form as half-man and half-lion. He ripped open the body of the demon by the sharp claws of the Lion-man. To situate the event to the proper context, it can be said that lion, being an animal of the forest, is the symbol of the unharnessed energy of the divine. That power of the Universe comes to the level of matter and creates the Lion-man. It also symbolizes a stage in Man's prowess.

UNIQUE FORMS

Animals are not only the earliest form of creatures but they are by far the most variable species living in varied ecological conditions of the Earth, the Water and the Sky. In the beginning the fish, the turtle and the boar emerged as life divine. Of the other animals some are connected with the event of creation and practically all are associated with the Hindu pantheon. Each form of animal divinities is unique in its generic character and behavioural qualities. The forms are innumerable.

Some animals find mention in ocean cosmology. During the time of churning the ocean of milk, Kamadhenu, the wish-fulfilling cow, appeared. Out of this also arose a milky white elephant with a huge body and two tusks.

This was Airavat. From this churning, the first white-headed horse, named Uccaisrava, appeared. The whole Universe is like an ocean. The supreme God, having devoured all beings, sleeps on the lap of the thousand-headed gigantic serpent known as Ananta or Shesha. The conch is the symbol of the origin of existence.

Some animals are sacred because the Gods took their form. Cow is the abode of every God and Goddess on Earth and Heaven. Shiva and Parvati took the form of elephants and lived in hills and mountains for ages, enjoying the delights of animal life. Buddha was once born as the son of an elephant having six tusks. Horse is described as a minor incarnation of Vishnu, as Hayegriva, horse-headed God. The Bodhisattva took the form of a winged horse. Vishnu is described as Ananta or Shesha, his animal determinant. The conch is his emblem.

Animals are the vehicles (*vahana*) of Gods. Shiva as Pashupati, the Lord of animals, rides a bull. Indra, the Rain God, rides on an elephant named Airavat. Agni, the Fire God, rides a blue ram. Vehicles of most of the Vedic Gods were drawn by horses. The Sun-God rides a seven-steads chariot. Kaliki, the incarnation yet to come, will also ride a horse. The lion is the vehicle of Durga. Garuda, the eagle-man, is the vehicle of Vishnu. The Moon God rides an antelope. Yama, the Lord of Death, rides a buffalo. The ass or donkey is one of the vehicles of Shitala, the Goddess of smallpox. The rat is the vehicle of Ganesha, the God who removes obstacles and bestows success. The peacock is the vehicle of Kartikeya, the War God. The vehicle of Kama, the God of venal love, is parrot. The owl is the vehicle of Lakshmi, the Goddess of wealth. The one-legged God Saturn rides a vulture and also an eagle. The swan is the vehicle of Brahma, it also became a vehicle of Vishnu when he assumed the traits of Brahma and later on of Saraswati, the Goddess of learning. Yamuna, a River Goddess, sits on a turtle. Another River Goddess Ganga stands on a crocodile. A cat is regarded as the charger of Shashti, the Goddess of fertility. The animal-mount of Vasundhara is a mongoose.

The concept of *vishwarupa*, the God of majesty and splendour with infinite forms of the Universe, has a reference to Vishnu. The notion of infinite forms and the belief that anthropomorphic and zoomorphic forms are capable of interchange led to the formation of composite forms. Shiva as Ardhanarishvara is both male and female; as Harihar he is half-Vishnu and half-Shiva. His son Ganesha is elephant-headed. His father-in-law Daksha has goat's head. The divine bird Garuda is a winged human figure. Fauns like the bull-man, the fish-tailed bull and the human-headed bull are sculpted in various parts of

India. There are also elephant-headed fish and elephant Makara (in the form of human and animal figures). In some representations, winged lions and lions with human head and having horned and beaked types are shown.

In their anthropomorphic forms, Gods are shown with many faces and many hands, signifying that they are more than humans. Asvins possess two heads. Brahma has four heads, representing four qualities of the Earth (the four faces are directed towards four directions) and four hands. Kartikeya is shown with six heads and twelve hands. Agni is represented with three heads and seven arms and three legs, symbolical of the creative heat of the Sun, preserving light and destroying Fire of the seven days of the week over which the Sun has its rule. Sarbha, one of the forms of Shiva, is eight-footed. Vishnu has four arms. In the form of Ananta, the World Serpent, he supported the Earth with the help of seven heads. Goddess have many hands but only one face. Durga has one face and eight or ten hands. Vasundhara has six arms and one face. Shiva has three eyes. As Pashupati he has five heads. Hanumana is sometimes shown as the five-faced Monkey God with ten hands. The Supreme Creator is described as a God of Gods with thousand eyes, thousand feet and thousand hands.

ANIMAL TWO MAN THREE

Animals have been given ontological priority in their perfection as well as their simplicity. Man comes only next in his original and primordial character. As God has assumed the powers of Brahman, so have the animals derived the quality and the powers of God. The cow represents the Goddess Lakshmi as the bestower of wealth, plenty and nourishment. The bull symbolizes the productive power of Nature. It represents the virile strength of Vishnu. Famed for its beauty, it is regarded as a symbol of self-control and resolution. The elephant symbolizes the life-giving force of Nature. It represents the power of faith. The horse is known for its breathtaking swiftness, its energy and strength. The lion is the king of beasts. Its majestic mien, strength, courage and its mighty terrifying roar have added to its prowess and glory. The boar is one of the brave and well-armed animals. Of the wild animals, the deer is known for its docility and inoffensive and gentle ways. The eyes of a deer are regarded as very beautiful. The jackal is a very cunning animal. The cat approaches its prey very silently and patiently. The hare is known to have noblest and self-sacrificing quality. The buffalo is an embodiment of sloth and laziness. It is admired for the quality of forbearance. It can also be a terror in the hearts of the people, as when provoked it can charge and create panic. The goat represents three qualities of Nature. A she-goat is the symbol of unmanifested Nature. The mouse or rat is the master of the insides of everything. It is the real enjoyer of the pleasure of all creatures. A mouse steals from people the thing they enjoy. Yet the mouse is not concerned whether those enjoyments are virtues or vices.

The peacock is the most glamorous bird. Its dance is symbolic of the awakening of Nature on the onset of rains. It is also admired for its ability to kill its enemy. The crow is regarded as soul animal. The eagle is known for its long-sightedness and keen vision. The crane is well-known for flying in long rows in the sky by way of expressing its joy in rain and downpour. The cock is an embodiment of fighting spirit. The swan exhibits in its habits and habitats, two aspects of nature of all living beings. Although it swims on the surface of the water, it is not limited to it. Withdrawing from its watery realm, it flies into the pure air. It also migrates from south to north and vice versa according to the change of the season. Thus, it is almost a free wanderer. In the spiritual context it has been described as macrocosmic gander, the divine Self in the body of the Universe. The swan is a symbol of sovereign freedom through stainless spirituality. There are a few other characteristics which make it a symbol of valued excellence. It likes to eat lotus. It has a beautiful gait and a sweet voice and the male bird is known for his sport with his partner. The swan is also attributed with the power of separating water from milk. It is regarded as the symbol of knowledge.

The snake has the capacity to move fast without legs and to live on land and in water. It is deadly poisonous. It has the ability to periodically shed its skin and grow a new one and has keen sense of audition and reputed ability to live on the air it breathes. On the turtle rests the earth. Its upper shell represents the sky, the lower shell represents the earth and in between the shells is the air. It draws in all its limbs. It is always delighted in soul. On the basis of this nature, it is regarded as a representative of the Supreme God, the universal Soul. The fish represents truth and transcendental wisdom, as it can cross and swim the seas, the world. The conch is associated with the primeval sound from which creation started. It represents the pure notion of individual existence. The ant is a social animal. It is believed that the first living beings were ants and that a second death after the first is possible in which the soul becomes an ant. Ants know about the weather and they also know when it will rain. If there are many ants in summer, it is believed, there will be a severe winter. Ants are symbols of endurance and hard work. They teach solemn modesty and humility. The scorpion is a nocturnal animal. It is a dangerous enemy of man but the poison it carries does not harm itself. Cannibalism is found in scorpions as they devour the young ones of their own kind. Fossil specimens of scorpions are similar to the present-day forms and are unchanged for billion years. Hence, modern scorpions are called 'living fossils'. The spider is also poisonous. In the evolution of animal life, spider has six legs. A spider makes a web and remains entangled in it for food and survival.

ANIMAL WEIRDNESS

Animals derive the powers from God. In some cases the position is reversed. It was with the help of Hanumana, the Monkey General of Sugriva's army of monkeys, that God Rama was able to vanquish Ravana and recover Sita. The *Ramayana* reveals Hanumana's extraordinary powers. Hanumana leaps across the sea to Lanka by making his body swell immensely. When he reaches Lanka he makes his body shrink so as to be inconspicuous. He becomes invisible. During the battle with Ravana, when Lakshmana faints, Hanumana takes a far mightier leap to the Himalayas, in the very far north, to bring life-restoring medicinal herbs. Unable to identify the specific herbs, he breaks off the entire crest of the hill, brings it to Lanka and revives Rama's brother Lakshmana. At Rama's bidding he returns to the Himalayas to restore the peak.

Rahu, the snake-like animal, harbours a hatred against the Sun and the Moon and it always tries to seize them. This explains the occurrence of solar and lunar eclipses from time to time. In the Hindu astrology, Rahu is described as the dragon's head and Ketu as the dragon's tail. They are respectively the ascending and the descending nodes or points where the ecliptic is crossed by the Moon. The dragon's head is dark and the dragon's tail is of muddy colour.

Of the twelve zodiacal signs, seven are animals. The Ram, the Bull, the heavenly Twins, the Crab, the Lion, the Virgin, the Scales, the Scorpion, the Archer, the She-Goat, the Water-Pot and the Fish represent respectively the head, face, breast, belly, navel, abdomen, genital organ, teeth, eyes, knees, anklets and the feet of *Kalapurusha* (the Time Person).

As vehicles of eight Dikpalas (Lord of quarters) are included the elephant (east), the buffalo (south), the crocodile (west), the man (north), the bull (north-east), the goat (south-east), the corpse (south-west) and the deer (north-west).

On the various superclusters of the Universe there is a Goloka, the World of Cow, which is divine and eternal. It is located above the three *lokas* (worlds).

Here there is no sickness, no old age, no death, no sorrow and no fear. All the six seasons remain here for ever. At the time of dissolution, the divine couple, Krishna and Radha stay here and at the time of creation this is filled by the cow herdsmen-and-women. Fifty crore *yojana* down the Goloka are located Vaikuntha (the abode of Vishnu) in the right direction and Shivaloka (the abode of Shiva) in the left direction. There is also the world of snake.

Taking an ontological view of all these and other examples of animal weirdness, the entire Universe can be seen as a living animal with enormous divine complexities.

POSITIVE SYMBIOSIS

Man is also a kind of animal (*pasu,* the 'roped' one). So are the Gods. Shiva is Pashupati, the Lord of Animals. But this does not suggest their physical similarities (homologies). Forms are different. All beings are 'roped' by the Law of birth-and-death. Hence *pasu.* Form comes from the formless. God is essentially formless but it can assume any form and many forms. In spiritual biology no species develop out of other species. The number of species is fixed. There are eighty-four billions of them within which humans, animals and divine rotate. In Hindu thought there is no path of evolution, no selection and no survival of the fittest in the Darwinian sense but interspecies transposition of the individual soul can be seen in terms of phylogeny at the biological level, especially when there is a movement from Animal to God. The reverse process is also at work in case God returns to the world of Man. Interspecies relationships, as actualized in liturgical and social (totemic) contexts can be seen as natural symbiosis.

The world of Man changes faster than the world of God. But this does not cause disequilibrium in the Universe, for whatever the difference in time biology, the life-pattern in the two worlds remains the same. The sages have said so:

> Whatever is here, that is there.
> What is there, that again is here.
> He obtains death after death.
> Who seems to see a difference here.
>
> —*Katha Upanisada* 4.9

By mind alone it is to be realized that there is no difference between this world and the other world. The two worlds make a suitable habitat for all life. The ontological concern of a living being is to maintain the original symmetry.

This world is an archetype of the other world. Man, Animal and God form an isosceles triangle on the surface of the Universe to which the God provides super-symmetry. Symmetry keeps the world going. This can be imagined from the symmetry that exists between the two opposites: male and female, positive and negative electric charge and north and south poles of a magnet.

In all that follows, Man cannot be the measure of all. The Animal seems to set standard for him. Man aspires for the productive power of a bull; the swiftness, energy and strength of a horse; the majestic mien and courage of a lion; the docility and inoffensiveness of a deer; the self-sacrificing quality of hare; the intelligence of an elephant; the keen sense of audition of a snake; the dance of a peacock; the beautiful gait and sweet voice of a swan; the solemn modesty and humility of an ant and so on. Since these attributes are the animal's transpersonal powers derived from God, it can be safely argued that all the three—Man, Animal and God—derive their attributes from a common source, the Cosmic Intelligence.

This thesis has an important consequence: Man-Animal relationship is based upon complementarity. The ancient sages had realized this. They did not merely chant the majesty of the cosmos and the glory of God, but they also lived in positive symbiosis with the animal world. The Vedic priest, for instance, sang the hymn as a blessing upon the cows:

> Abound in calves, graze on good pastures,
> drinking pure water at the springs.
> Owned neither by thief nor by wicked man,
> may you be spared the darts of Rudra!
> May this potion, enhanced by the seed of the Bull
> and by your power, O Indra, bring these Cows fertility.
>
> —*Rigveda* VI.7-88

India is a cow-land. Cow is the *sattvika* symbol for all animals. A cow is not only worshipped, its five products (milk, curd, melted clarified butter, dung and urine) are used as a means of cleansing sins. Giving away a cow is an important ritual at the time of death. The dying person holds the tail of a cow which is a symbolic act of crossing the dreadful river Vaitarni on way to the heavenly abode. The cow leads the dead Man to the Heaven and absolves him of all the sins that he has committed during his lifetime. Cows are worshipped as a means of counteracting the flows or signs of bad luck indicated in the horoscope; rebirth from a cow is simulated.

To maintain interspecies symmetry and to establish the Law (*Dharma*), God Vishnu is born in every age. In his incarnation as Rama, he made friendship with monkeys and bears. In the form of Krishna he was known as Gopala, the cow-protector. And in the form of Buddha he lived with the deer and preached non-violence to all animals.

The cow is the measure of ontological change in the moral order of Time. Metaphorically speaking, in the Kritayuga (or Golden Age), the Cow of *Dharma* stood on four legs; in the Treta (the next age) she rested on three legs; in the Dvapara (the third age) she stood on two legs; and in the Kali (the modern age) she is limping on one leg alone. The central thrust is clear: the virtue declines in time. We live in the age of Kali (darkness); the cow of our moral order is limping.

Animals have influenced the Hindu thought to such a degree that they form the core of human consciousness—sensual, intellectual and mystical, all in one. Animal symbols are used as instruments of knowing the unknowable. The mystery of the Self is expressed with profound wisdom.

Like a she-goat, *Prakriti* (Nature) comprises three qualities that give birth to the world. First to be born is the universal intellect. Some of the he-goats, after enjoying the spotted she-goat whose children are likewise spotted, still follow her while others, having enjoyed her, abandon her. So also some living beings, after enjoying Nature, follow her who, spotted with the three qualities, procreates the world, while others, having enjoyed her, proceed towards another goal.

Every pervading *Atman* (Soul) is the mouse, which lives in the hole of intellect within the heart of every being. Like the mouse, this Self of all beings is a thief because, unnoticed, it steals away all that people possess. It hides itself behind the inscrutable shape of illusion and no one knows that this inner ruler takes for himself the pleasures which they believe they enjoy.

Vedic astrology illustrates a basic insight of mutual relationship determined by the asterism at birth. The genital characteristics ascribed to asterisms, that is *yoni,* which literally means the organ of reproduction in the female, is a point in which there should be an agreement in the horoscope of two persons, especially of the bride and the bridegroom. This works as follows: Aswini and Sathabis—Horse; Bharani and Revathi—Elephant; Pushya and Krittika—Sheep; Rohini and Mrigasirsha—Serpent; Aslesha and Punarvasu—Cat; Magha and Purvaphalguni—Rat; Uttaraphalguni, Uttarashadha and Uttarabhadrapada—Cow; Swathi and Hastha—Buffalo; Vaisakha and Chaitra—Tiger; Jyeshta and Anuradha—Deer; Mula and Ardha—Dog; Purvashada and Sravana—Monkey;

Sraivishta and Purvabhadrapada—Lion. Of these, monkey and sheep, deer and elephant, horse and buffalo, cow and tiger, rat and cat, serpent and rat, serpent and mongoose, dog and deer are mutually hostile—so inauspicious. To show suitability the asterisms of the couple should be of the same *yoni*. If different, it is neutral; hostile *yoni* should be avoided. The implication of this belief is that Man on the Earth is intrinsically inseparable from Animal to an extent that his interpersonal relationship within the species is patterned by animal characteristics.

Chapter 2

The Order of Nature

THE SACRED NUMBERS

In Indian cosmological thought, the number appears as the great instrument of explanation.. The structure of the Universe is measured in terms of 0, 1, 2, 3. The Threefold pattern occurs at every level of manifestation. From the Cosmic Egg, symbolizing zero (fullness), originates the Three forms of life (God, Animal, Man), the Threefold geometric concept designating Threefold knowledge (centre *Yajurveda*, diameter *Rigveda*, circumference *Samaveda*) and the Threefold pattern of metamorphosis (creation, existence, dissolution). The Cosmic Egg has Three superclusters of Universes (Earth, middle region, Sky) called microcosm, mesocosm and macrocosm. The Universe of matter has Three qualifying factors (light, energy, inertia); their equilibrated condition is called Nature. Creation is the result of tension among the Three factors. The cosmological state of dissolution remains in dynamic equilibrium with the universal bodies.

As an instrument of knowledge, the number assumes power and sacredness. One of the wondrous features of the sacred number is its unlimited qualifying character. It forms the basic strands around which the fabric of the Universe is woven. The sacred number is not a mathematical thought number but it is as valid as Euclidean geometry. As a symbol of natural language, the number Three embraces all; it goes back to the early history of Man. Among the Onge of the Andaman Islands, for example, Three is the absolute number. For all categories of relations in the third and subsequent generations, they have common term. Father, mother and child form a natural triad in human intuition. The Christian traid of Father, Son and Holy Spirit is plainly discernible. But when sacredness is extended beyond Three, this explanation does not work.

Of the sacred numbers, Four, Five, Six, Seven, Eight and Nine are related to and consistent with the other symbologies of cosmological structures. For instance, the Four-faced Brahma, archetypal Dean of creation, enunciates the

Vedic knowledge in a Fourfold pattern or evolves the cosmos as a *swastik* with Four angles of 90° each. The Four faces are aligned to the Four directions. The mother cow Viraj in whose body all the divine power abides, has Four udders for streams of milk by which she supports Four kinds of creatures (sages, ancestors, gods and men). The Four cosmic ages, signifying the Four categories of moral and spiritual orders, represent the Fourfold scheme of creation. The Four-footed Brahman has been conceived in terms of the Four Vedas, the Four castes of men and the Fourfold scheme existing for ever. The Five-faced Shiva symbolizes the Five material elements, the Five oblations offered into Five fires, the Five sense organs, the Five causal sounds, the Five categories of Soul and the Five evolving modalities of the one transcendent reality. The group of Six names of Fire is terrific in nature. Originally Fire was one but differentiated for the sake of different rites. The Sevenfold scheme within the Cosmic Egg gives the Seven Great Ones, the Seven Worlds, the Seven Islands, the Seven Seas, the Seven Mountains, the Seven types of Air in Seven Shells around the Earth. The Eight forms of Rudra or Shiva symbolize the Five gross material elements, plus the Two opposite principles of Heat and Cold and the Mind. The Fires in the Soma sacrifice are Eight in number. There are Eight protecting divinities. The worship of the Nine planets is called *navagraha-makha*. The Nine divisions of ancient India find mention in the *Puranas*.

The sacred number can thus be considered a signature for universal qualities. By assuming sacred power the individual number is so transformed that it remains neither mathematical nor purely cultural. Standing outside the temporal context, the sacred number is a reflexive expression, a universal distribution of ideas attributed to self-structured cosmic knowledge (*ritambharara pranjna*). Its major function is to reduce the spatial, temporal, cultural and personal diversities in human thought so that the fundamental form of relations and articulations between Man and his Universe is concretized.

THE LIVING MATTER

The Vedic cosmology comes out of a profound insight into the mystery of the Universe. The sages began by a series of negatives. The Golden Germ revealed itself.

With the affirmation of 'divine life', the Cosmic Person (*Purusa*) emanates and performs an act of self-sacrifice. From this sacrifice come all things, both animate and inanimate: animals of every type, liturgical formulas, the Four castes of men and the cosmic powers.

The Moon was born from his mind;
the Sun came into being from his eyes;
from his mouth came Indra and Agni,
while from his breath the Wind was born.

From his navel issued the Air;
from his head unfurled the Sky,
the Earth from his feet, from his ear the four directions.
Thus have the worlds been organized.

—*Rigveda* X, 90

The origin of the Five Elements—Water, Fire, Air, Sky, Earth—from the void in the world and darkness engulfing all around can be compared with the modern scientific view of the origin of world out of the Black Hole state of the matter. The Vedic sages seem to have arrived at this notion through, what is called in Indian intellectual tradition, *yogic pratyaksha,* an advanced stage of thought experimentation. The modern view in earth sciences presupposes a great cloud of slowly rotating hot gaseous material as the starting point of the Universe. As this cloud cooled, it shrank and rotated more rapidly. The cloud got gradually compressed at polar regions into a lens-shaped disc which gradually let off masses of gases which cooled down first to a liquid state and then to solid state, giving rise to planets.

According to the revealed texts (*Srutis*), Water appears to be the First Element. It is an animating cosmic element, a primordial liquid, vivifying organism. It is the first need of a living creature, a basic factor of existence. Out of the Five Elements, Fire may be regarded as a dominating Element. It transcends its physical character. It is indicative of immortality. The Vedic sages recognized Air as a vital cosmic constituent. It is the soul of sacrifice, a source of health, happiness and long life. The breath is the vital form of Air. Sky is identified with the Soul, with *Purusa*, with Prajapati and with Brahman.

The *Taittiriya Upanisada* traces the evolution of living matter. From this Soul (*Atman*), Space (Sky); from Space, Wind; from Wind, Fire; from Fire, Water; from Water, the Earth; from the Earth, herbs; from herbs, food; from food, semen; from semen, the person. The life or person is constituted by the Five sheaths (*kosa*): the field of food (*annamaya-kosa*), the field of life (*pranamaya-kosa*), the field of mind (*manomaya-kosa*), the field of knowledge (*vijnanmaya-kosa*) and the field of bliss (*anandamaya-kosa*).

Like the seers of the Vedas and the *Upanisadas*, the 'tribes' of North-Eastern India have perceived the deep mysteries in the vast and variegated world. Their cosmogonic myths correspond with the views of the Vedic and *upanisadic* cosmology. They also believe that matter is the field of life. There is a Fivefold Order that sets forth the timeless sequence of creation, existence and dissolution. The First Order is set in nothingless: 'In the beginning there was nothing, nothing at all but Water, or clouds and mist, or two Eggs soft and shone like gold. In that state, life was there above the primeval Water, hidden deep in the clouds and mists, or in the two whirling eggs. With such vibration of life, the beginning was not an absolute vacuity'. The Second Order causes primary creation of Elements from the Elements of the First Order. The First creation was asexual. The Golden Eggs collided and both broke open. From the one came the Earth and from the other the Sky. Subsequently, creation became a male-female principle. When the Sky made love to Earth, every kind of tree, grass and all living creatures came into being. The world was created in phases by a number of vibrant bodies and not by a single creator. The order of creation began with the formless spirits and then the Sun-Moon and all the rest. At first there were two or four or eight or nine suns of an unbearable brightness. The radiance of one of them was gradually reduced to the cool and gentle light of the Moon. The early phases of creation were marked by total integration of all that exists; there was no difference between Man and non-Man. Every Element has its own life. Elements of Nature are inter-related. What activates or transforms matter is the transcendent life; but life itself is not matter. The Third Order causes natural identity and differentiation in terms of colour, direction and form. Smell is another element of the Third Order; it makes communication between the form and the formless possible. The Fourth Order causes the return to primordial state. Water is the self-existing element from which all other elements originate and to which they all return. The Fifth Order is the Order of all orders. It creates a scenario of the world in which everything has a place and everything grows and allows others to grow.

THE FIVEFOLD ORDER

The notion of nothingness is realized both in 'tribal' myth and the *upanisadic* science. Both trace the evolution of the living matter. Both realize that the elements of matter are subject to a Fivefold order: Origination, Binding, Interlocking, Overlapping and Transcending.

ORIGINATION

A parallel of the tribal Golden Germ can be found in the Vedic description of

Hiranyagarbha. The myth of the Earth, the Cosmic Mother, dying of her own accord and becoming the part of the world, is close to the Vedic *Purusa*, the Cosmic Man, who performed an act of self-immolation so that the Universe could come into being. Three apparent ideas emerge: break in the radical solidarity gave origin to life; heterogeneity is a fundamental aspect in the origin and development of species; and built-in-order of cosmic unity as 'one and many'.

Binding

Elements of Nature have a building ability. Each Element has a form, a location and a dependent-relation with another Element. Living forms of Nature are self-originating, self-organizing and self-sustaining. Form is predetermined; it is filled by perishable matter. Life is formless, self-existent and, essentially, indestructible. As form and life come together, the process of origination begins. Life activates matter that constitutes form, but in itself is not a material substance. Elements constitute human and other forms, both individually and collectively. Each major organ is said to have its own builder. Head and ears are associated with the Sky; neck and chest with Air; stomach with Fire; and body with Earth. Elements are also known to have caused the origin of bio-social types. The blacksmiths relate themselves with Earth, carpenters with Water, coppersmiths with Fire, sculptors with Wind and goldsmiths with Sky. The *Garbha Upanisada* describes life-processes thus: One night after the union in a fertile period, arises a nodule (*kalia*); after seven nights it changes into bubble (*budbud*); in half a month arises the embryo (*pinda*); after one month it becomes solid; when two months have passed, the head appears; after three months the formation of the feet is completed; at four months happily originates the sex, the abdomen and the hips; at five months the back forms; after six months form the mouth, nose, eyes and ears; and after seven months the individual soul concludes the unification. At eight months all the parts are complete.

If the tribal description of Elements constituting human form is transposed on the *upanisadic* theory, it would be clear that both hold the same view. The liquid stage from which the embryo arises is Water; when the embryo becomes solid it is Earth; the appearance of hollow head is Sky; the formation of the moving feet is Wind; the origination of sex and abdomen is associated with heat or Fire. This sequence of embryonic development roughly corresponds with the origin of the Universe—from primeval Water to Earth and Sky and from these two Wind and Fire. It also supports the general theory of Man as microcosm.

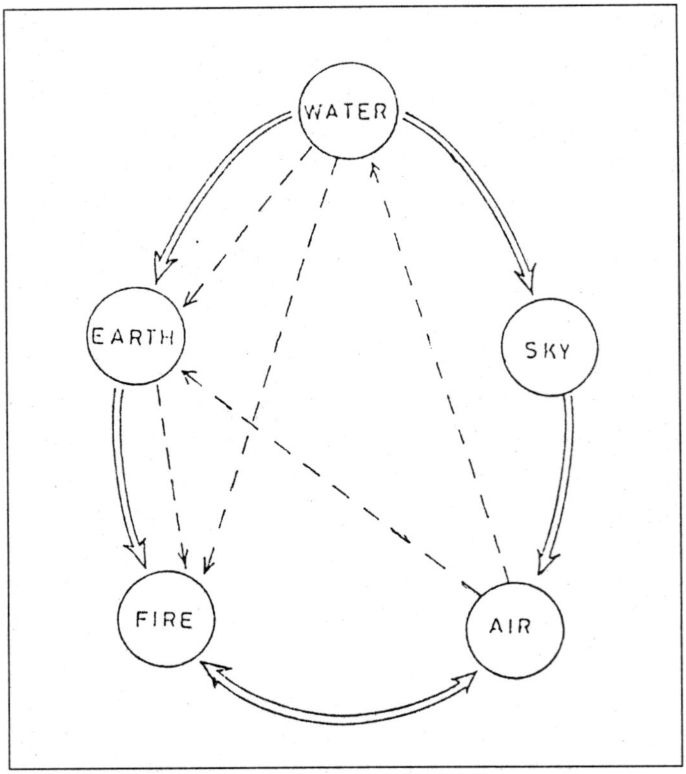

Fig. 1. Interlocking Elements
⇒Positive ------→ Negative

Interlocking

Form and life are cross-linked. By entering into a form, the formless life acquires qualitative distinctions. It gives different expressions to different forms or species. Accordingly, it is called by different names. As a transcendent substance, life gets involved in the threefold cosmic process of formation (origination), affirmation (preservation) and negation (dissolution) of Elements. Interlocking of life and form helps realize the existential changes; it makes Cosmic Order visible. Interlocking of Elements is described metaphorically: Earth and Sky are universal parents; Fire and Air are brothers just as Water and Mist are brothers. Earth and Air, Water and Fire are negatively linked; they have always been enemies. Air is the friend of Fire against Water and he fights the rain to drive it before him (Fig.1). The more complex interlocking is perceived in the Ayurveda (Fig.2). The Five primal Elements are linked with other Elements or aspects of Nature such as colour, form, sense organ, physical character, property, functions, etc. These Elements are also linked with psychological attributes called *guna*. Further, each Element is associated with divinity and its related aspects such as *mantra*, etc.

Overlapping

Elements have both personal (material) and universal (spiritual) attributes. In 'tribal' cosmology, Water and Egg, which appeared in the beginning, have a fundamental feature of sacredness. The other primal Elements such as Earth,

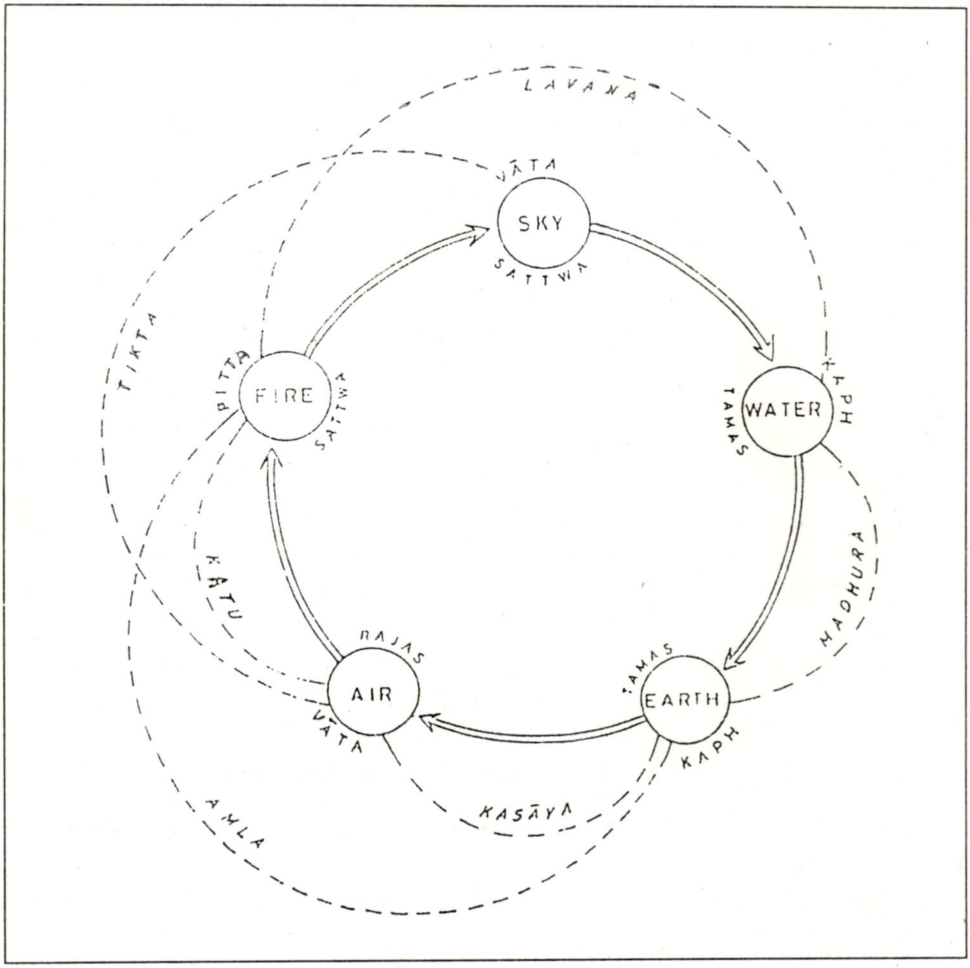

Fig. 2. Interlocking Elements (Ayurvedic Tradition)
5 *Elements*, 3 *Gunas*, 3 *Dosas*, 3 *Rasas*

⇒Interlocking Path ------→ Composition of *Rasas*

Air, Fire and Sky (with the Sun, Moon and Stars) have also a similar indwelling sacred attributes. However, not all the Elements are spiritually vibrant all the time and at all places; but they can be made so in a ritual way. The Elements exist in two overlapping spheres—material and spiritual—simultaneously with different ranges of Time and Space. The world is divided into two halves—the Sky and the Earth. There is a world beyond the Sky and another below the Earth. The Earth is a round-shaped flat surface; the Sky is a hollow concave, overarching the Earth. The Five Elements overlap in their formation and so also the world of matter with the other worlds. Life in this world is repeated

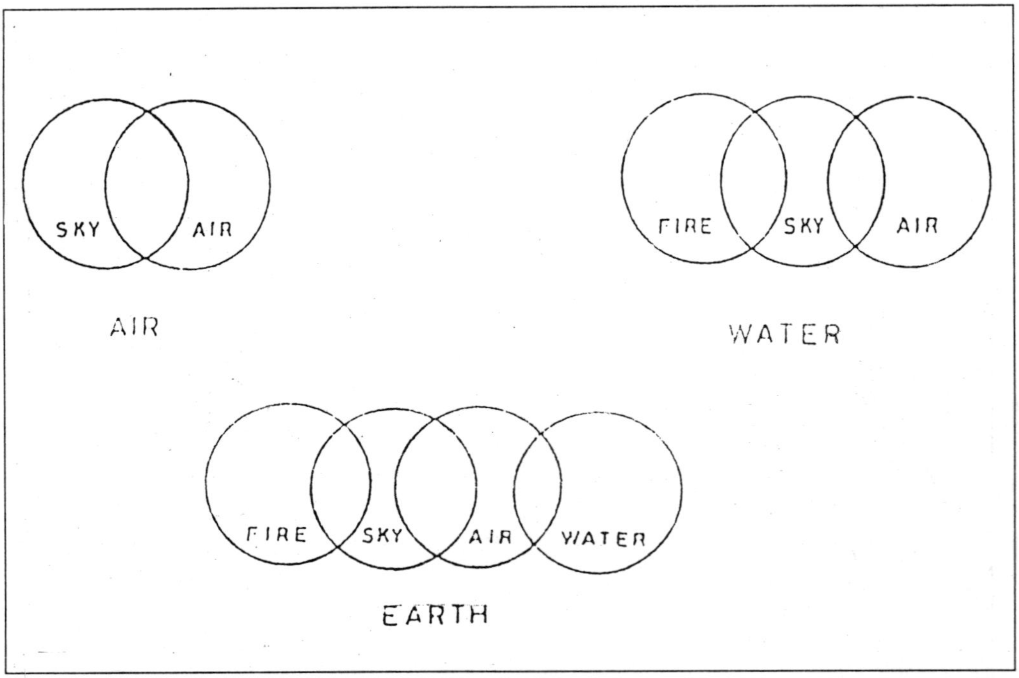

Fig. 3. Overlapping Elements
Eternal (*parmanu*) Forms
(a) *dwyanuka* (b) *trayanuka* (c) *caturnuka*

in the other world in a similar order. Worlds are communicable in dream and trance.

According to the Vaisesika system of philosophy, the Five Elements overlap in their formation. There are three evolutionary states: *bhuta, mahabhuta* and *drishyabhuta.* The *bhuta* is the atomic state, which is eternal. When two atoms (*paramanu*) combine, it is called diatonic (*dwyanuka*); when three diatonics combine, it becomes triatonic (*trasarenu*); and in the like manner, the four diatonics also combine. It is at this state that grossness appears and as such it begins to be known as *mahabuta.* The triatonic of the Sky Element combines with that of the Air and gives rise to the Air *mahabhuta.* Similarly, Sky, Air and Fire are in the Water *mahabhuta a*nd the Earth *mahabhuta* contains all the four *mahabhutas* (Fig.3). The process of regressive intrusion is called *anupravesh,* after which all the *mahabhutas* attain their normal position. For creating the material objects they all combine together again in varying proportions and thus material Element (*drishyabhuta*) is formed. In each case there is predominance of one or the other *mahabhuta* on which basis the character of the objects is defined as Earth, Water, etc. For instance, when an object is

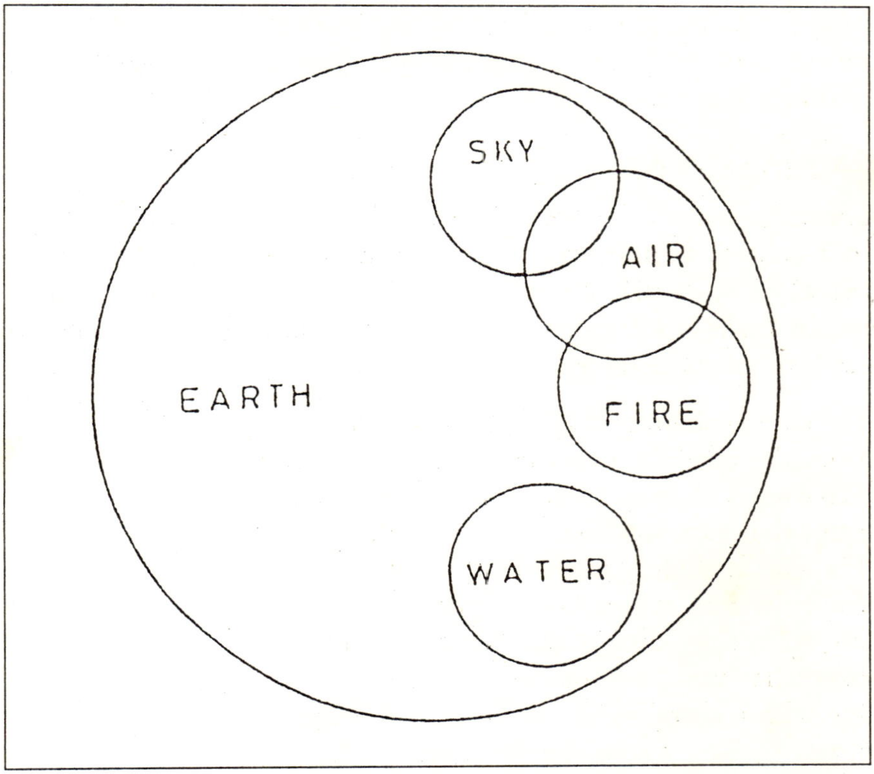

Fig. 4. Overlapping Elements
Gross Earth containing 50 per cent earth and in the residue all the remaining four elements

called Earth it does not mean that it is composed of Earth alone. It means it is composed of all the *mahabhutas* wherein the Earth *mahabhuta* is predominant. Generally, the predominant *mahabhuta* is 50 per cent and in the residual portion all the remaining four take their equal share (Fig.4).

TRANSCENDING

Cosmogonic myths of North-East India describe how the limits of the natural state are transcended. The state of primordial solidarity was transcended when the two whirling Eggs broke open and the Universe revealed itself. The Order of origination was transcended by the male-female principle. The Order of self-organization was transcended by the interlocking of various Elements. The spatial order of the pluriverse was transcended by the overlapping of spheres in dream and trance. Life transcends the limits of the form. Death transcends all attributes of Elements, including the limits of the terrestrial Time. Yet, there is no intrinsic disorder in Nature. Dissolution is the integral aspect of the Nature's transcendent Order. Transcendence is the Order of all Orders; it is inviolable.

THE INTEGRAL VISION

The *upanisadic* sages had a total vision of the Elements of the Universe. They were not concerned only with the physical or spiritual, or with the merely allegorical or spiritual, but with the integral experience of reality. The *Upanisadas* make no division between matter and spirit. The Elements are the real symbol standing for the higher reality:

> He who is abiding in the Earth, yet different
> from the Earth, whom the Earth does not know....
> He who is abiding in the Waters, yet different
> from the Waters, whom the Waters do not know....
> He who is abiding in the Fire, yet different
> from the Fire, whom the Fire does not know...
> He who is dwelling in the Wind, yet different
> from the Wind, whom the Wind does not know...
> He who is dwelling in the Sky, yet different
> from the Sky, whom the Sky does not know...
>
> —*Brihadaranyaka Upanisada* III.7

That whose body is the Element, who controls the Elements from within, is the Soul, the inner controller, the Immortal. The Five Elements find reflection in several texts concerning the various aspects of the human adventure.

THE AYURVEDIC TRADITION

The Five Elements are perceived in the Ayurveda in terms of their property, physical character, association with sense objects, functions and psychological property (*guna* or *dosa*). They constitute the living animal body and the vegetable and mineral kingdoms. While the *mahabhutas* are the physical basis of the body, the *dosas* are their biological representatives responsible for physiological functions in the state of homoeostasis and for pathological disorders in the state of imbalance, given in Table 1.

The *guna* is located in the matter, or *dravya,* inherently. It is causative agent devoid of property and action, but it qualifies the *dravya* for such action. As a spiritual quality or psychological property, it is three in number: *sattva, rajas* and *tamas*. But as a physical attribute there are six *gunas*: heavy (*guru*), light (*laghu*), hot (*usna*), dry (*ruksa*) and wet (*snigdha*). Consideration of the six *gunas* in relation to the six *rasas* is very important from the applied physiological point of view. In the Ayurveda, *rasa* is the object of the gustatory sense organ which is located in the tongue. Each *rasa* is composed of two gross elements. The *madhura rasa* is composed of Earth and Water; *amla* of Earth and Fire; *lavana* of Water and Fire; *katu* of Air and Fire; *tikta* of Air and Sky; and *kasaya* of Air and Earth. The composition of *rasas* has been defused by inference on the basis of their effect. There are three *dosas*, each concerned with the combination of gross elements. Water and Earth are characterized by *kapha dosa;* Sky and Air by *vata dosa*; and Fire alone has *pitta dosa.* Interlocking of *gunas, dosas* and *rasas* and the Five Elements has been shown before (Fig. 2).

TABLE 1: THE FIVE ELEMENTS IN THE AYURVEDA

Element	*Sky*	*Air*	*Fire*	*Water*	*Earth*
Property	sound	touch	form	taste	smell
Physical character	absence of resistance	movement	heat	liquidity	roughness
Sensory organ	ears	skin	eyes	tongue	nose
Function	porousness, distinction	lightness, activity	colour, digestion, bravery, brightness, intolerance	heaviness coldness, oleaginous, semen	solidity, heaviness
Psychological property (*guna*)	*sattva*	*rajas*	*sattva*	*tamas*	*tamas*
Psychological property (*dosa*)	*vata*	*vata*	*pitta*	*kapha*	*kapha*

In line with the Ayurveda, the Five Elements theory is basic to Chinese medicine. They refer to Wood, Fire, Earth, Metal and Water. Their relationships are usually demonstrated in the following way: Fire burns Wood, which becomes ashes and these eventually become part of the Earth, in which Metal is found. When metal is melted, it becomes to all appearances Water (i.e. liquid) and Water nourishes everything which grows, including trees which in turn give us Wood and so on. In terms of disease, the Five Elements' structure is used to characterize various diseases and the ways in which they are cured or in which they attack human beings. Based upon the observed harmonies and disharmonies of the Five Elements, the Chinese doctors explain much of their treatment. The recurring cycle of Five is a frequent one in Chinese culture. The Five Elements affect both Nature (Table 2) and Man (Table 3).

TABLE 2: THE FIVE ELEMENTS THAT AFFECT NATURE

Element	*Wood*	*Fire*	*Earth*	*Metal*	*Water*
Natural development	birth	growth	transformation	collection	storage
Colour	green	red	yellow	white	black
Taste	sour	bitter	sweet	metallic	salty
Season	spring	summer	late summer	autumn	winter
Climate	windy	hot	humid	dry	cold

TABLE 3: THE FIVE ELEMENTS THAT AFFECT MAN

Element	*Wood*	*Fire*	*Earth*	*Metal*	*Water*
Yin organs	liver	heart	spleen	lungs	kidneys
Yang organs	gall-bladder	small intestine	stomach	large intestine	bladder
Body tissue	tendon	blood vessels	muscle	skin, hair	bone
Sensory organs	eyes	tongue	mouth	nose	ears
Emotions	anger	joy, excitement	anxiety	grief	fear

In considering the nature of the body, the Chinese theory of *yin* and *yang* (see Table 4) has to be understood. Everything in the Universe is either *yin* or *yang*—the world itself, the objects in the world, mankind, the parts of the body, the functions of those parts and the medical conditions which affect those functions. Neither *yin* nor *yang* is absolute. Both are always changing. *Yin* can become *yang* and *yang* can become *yin*, according to the flux of the Universe. Nothing in this world is fixed and immutable. *Yin* is associated with heart, liver, spleen, lungs and kidneys. *Yang* joins small intestine, gall-bladder, stomach, large intestine and bladder.

TABLE 4: *YIN* AND *YANG* PHYSIOLOGY AND PATHOLOGY

Physiology

Sex	*Body Parts*	*Tissues and Organs*	*Condition/Function*
Yin Female	internal abdomen	blood, tendons, bone, heart, liver, spleen, lungs, kidneys	sedation, chronic, hypo-functional, degenerative
Yang Male	external back	energy, skin, hair, small intestine, stomach, gall-bladder, large intestine, bladder	stimulation, acute, hyper-function, generative

Pathology

Disease	Pulse
Yin Cold, internal, chronic, deficient, degenerative, hypo-functional	deep, slow, weak, deficient
Yang Hot, external, acute, excess, generative, hyper-functional	superficial, fast, strong, excess

THE RITUALISTIC TRADITION

The *Agamas* have visualized the Five Elements in a special way. The most important ritual is the element of purification (*bhutasuddhi*) meant for the devotee's unification with the divinity. Each Element is purified by inhalation and exhalation. Purification of that body is performed by bathing in the water. This is known as the eightfold form of Shiva. Bath with Five gross Elements is considered essential for the worshipper who makes use of clay, water, sacred ashes, dust that emerges from the feet of cows and the water fallen from the sky. The following order of worship is prescribed: invocation of Air that dries up the body, Fire that reduces to ashes, Water that freshens and purifies existence, Earth that brings the celestial body into full existence, Shiva-Shakti to charge the body with energy and the *mantra* to place the celestial existence back into the initial *cakra*. The desired deity is propitiated with five kinds of offerings. One offers sandal paste representing the Earth, flowers representing the Sky, incense representing the Air, lamp representing the Fire and food representing the Water. All these ritualistic offerings are meant to achieve confidence in oneself and to mark complete merger with the deity.

The five subtle domains of human body correspond with the Five Elements and the Five Gods:

Skull—Sky—Sadashiva
Eyebrows—Wind—Ishvara
Palate—Fire—Rudra
Throat—Water—Vishnu
Heart—Earth—Brahma

The intrinsic connection between the individual and the supreme Shiva is symbolically explained as follows: The two hands are considered not merely as limbs but as Shiva and Shakti, with the five fingers, from the little to the thumb, representing, respectively, Earth, Fire, Air, Water and Sky. In the ritualistic contexts, the objects are looked at not as inert matter but supercharged with divinity. Each gross element has a form and a colour of its own, each potentialized by a particular letter, activized by a deity and controlled by a supreme Lord. The Five Elements are related with several other characters (Table 5).

TABLE 5: THE FIVE ELEMENTS IN THE *AGAMAS*

Element	*Sky*	*Air*	*Fire*	*Water*	*Earth*
Form	circle	hexagon	triangle	half-moon	square
Symbol	point	six dots	*swastika*	lotus	*vajra*
Colour	pure crystal	black	red	white	yellow
Potentializing letter	*ha*	*ya*	*ra*	*va*	*la*
Activizing deity	Sadashiva	Maheshvara	Rudra	Vishnu	Brahma
Supreme lord	Ishana	Tatpurusa	Aghora	Vamadeva	Sadyojata
Bija-mantra	*haum*	*hyaim*	*hrum*	*hvim*	*halam*
Kala	*santyatita*	*santi*	*vidya*	*pratistha*	*nivrti*
Nature	void	mobile	hot	fluid	hard
Cosmic cow	Sumana (*citra varna*)	Sushila (*sveta varna*)	Surabhi (*rakta varna*)	Bhadra (*krsna varna*)	Nanda (*kapila varna*)

The five great causal sounds made at the termination of night are related to the Five Elements:

Sky	—	Sound born of songs (*geya*)
Air	—	Sound born of flute (*vamsa*)
Fire	—	Sound born of metal instrument (*lohaja*)
Water	—	Sound born of conch (*sankha*)
Earth	—	Sound born of wooden instrument (*daruja*)

The causal sounds ward off inauspiciousness and make all the deities content and happy.

There are sixteen kinds of services (*upacaras*) offered to the Lord at the end of worship. These are classified into five in relation to the Five Elements. In the course of the service, fourteenth is music (*geya*) and the fifteenth is dance (*nritya*). These two are related to the Sky Element. Just as there is no greater element than Sky, so also there is no service more effective and auspicious than music and dance. The *agamic* scriptures prescribe a particular *raga* to the particular division of a day. For example, every morning *gandharva*, the next division *malava raga*, midday *takka raga*, the next division *kaushika*, evening *hrindola* and night *pancam*.

THE MUSICAL TRADITION

Both *Paniniya Siksa*, a text dealing with phonetics and *Sangita-Ratnakara*, a musical text, describe speech, recitation and music in respect of the human body which is considered the primary source of sound. In the production of sound, Fire and Air are the main agents and Sky provides the requisite space for the action of Fire and the movement of Air. The Earth forms the base in the region below the navel. This, of course, is a figurative or indirect way of exposition. The terms standing for the qualities of the human voice are analyzed in respect of their association with the Five Elements: *madhur* (sweet) is associated with Water, because of the sense of taste; *ghana* (dense) with Earth, as density is its attribute; *snigdha* (creamy) and *rakta* (red or delighting) with Fire and Sky, the most basic and pervasive Element, has not been mentioned directly.

Music being directly related to aural and this perception being an attribute of Sky, is primarily related to the same. Conceptually, this relationship is complete in itself. But in the production, communication and enjoyment of musical sound, the other Four Elements have their definite roles. Water is related to the pattern of music. The qualities of the musical voice have been given figurative names that bear close affinity with one or the other of the Five Elements.

When Elements are spoken of as being Three, instead of Five, then Fire stands for energy in sound production, *tejomayi vak*, Earth stands for mind that propels energy and Water signifies life. Also terms for higher and lower notes are related to the impact of musical sound. *Dipta* (brilliant) is figuratively associated with Fire and *mridu* (soft or clear) could be related to Water. *Rasa* (taste), which embodies the culmination of aesthetic enjoyment, is the ultimate decisive factor of propriety in artistic creativity; it is directly related to Water.

The concept of space in dance relates to Earth and Sky. The breath of life is controlled by the dancer according to the needs of the movements at any particular given situation. Water, which forms a major ingredient of life, is thrown out as an excretion in the form of perspiration when excessive heat, a form of Fire, is produced due to strain while dancing. The various texts, starting from the *Natyasastra* onwards, give innumerable hand usages (*hastaviniyoga*) when referring to various aspects, such as:

Air	—	breeze, storm
Fire	—	heat, burning, flame, etc.
Sky and Earth	—	the movement of the body below the waist

It may be mentioned that Sky and Earth have a very special reference in dance literature. Bharata has used the terms *akasiki* (related to the Sky) and *bhumi* (related to the Earth) with reference to the *caris*. *Caris* done on the gound without raising the feet are referred to as *bhumi* and *caris* performed with one or both the feet moving in space (may be, even to a small measure, above the ground) is *akasiki*. The term *akasa* has been used for any space which is not on the ground.

THE FORM AND THE FORMLESS

The Hindu approach to form (*rupa*) involves a highly complex reflection. The pure knowledge of form is inwardly conceived. At the state of Element, the pure matter is formless. Form lies hidden in matter. But as soon as grossness appears, the *mahabhuta* is attributed with a tangible form. The concepts of form and formless, manifest and unmanifest, have fascinated the ancient thinkers.

The *agamic* tradition speaks of the five-headed Shiva, each representing one of the Five Elements. There are sacred places for each of the five forms of Shiva in South India:

Kanchipuram	—	*Prthvilingam* (Earth)
Jambukeshwaram	—	*Apulingam* (Water)
Arunachalam	—	*Tejolingam* (Fire)
Kalahasti	—	*Vayulingam* (Air)
Chidambaram	—	*Akashalingam* (Sky)

The five *lingas* are thus perceived as physical *akasha* or spaces. In other words, all Elements are essentially *akasha* in their subtle forms. There is another set of five *akashas* called *andhakaraksha, parakasha, mahakasha, suryakasha a*nd *paramakasha*. The Sky possesses the property of sound, i.e. it is made up of 'sound particles'. This means, within the 'outer space'. There is an 'inner space' (*hridyakasha*) called 'sound space' which cannot be seen but can be only heard or experienced inside.

As the Tamil grammar *Nannool* explains, 'sound particles' cluster together and grow into a definite form of *akasha* or uttered syllable (vowels and consonants). Form is the property of Fire, but luminosity itself is the quality of Sky. Hence the subtle luminous form is the Ultimate. Brahman is described as 'flame without smoke'.

To give another expression: *Om* is the primary sound or 'sound particle' which gradually develops into sound form. Every physical word (*vak*) has a physical form (*artha*), which originates not from '*Om* sound' but from '*Om* light'. The light *Om* is the source of all visual phenomena and the sound *Om* is the source of all aural phenomena. As allegorically stated, form is centrally situated in the light. This goes well with the concept of Shiva as a dancer encircled by a series of flames (*prabhamandal*).

The Hindu theory of form develops in yet another context. The absolute time has no past-present-future. It is ever present, ever active and ever pulsating. It springs from the 'inner' and the 'outer' spaces of every being. The Earth, as an organic form, also pulsates like a human being. There are three phenomenal sequences: thought at the level of 'inner space', the vibration of the 'inner space' with the urge to give form to the thought of consciousness and finally the resultant form called *vastu* or *pratima*. The process of vibration of the inner being to forge into a form is a subtle but vital principle. This is the creative elemental force emerging from within the space without immense force (a kind of atomic explosion). For easy understanding, the vibrations of inner being can be compared to the vibrations of the stringed instrument which at the other end emerges into a musical form worthy of enjoyment.

GEOMETRICAL FORMS

Following the *agamic* characterization of elements, Earth is represented by square, Water by crescent, Fire by triangle, Air by hexagon and Sky by circle. In the Vedic tradition, Sky is the ultimate because all things have arisen out of Sky and they all disappear back into Sky. The Earth is also eulogized as the dwelling from which life springs and to which it returns. This concern of giving equal importance to Earth and Sky suggests that square and the circle are the basic geometrical forms.

Following the *Shilpasastra,* within the square frame and the space of a circle, a whole cosmos is contained. In the *agamic* tradition, as stated earlier, all elements are essentially Sky in their subtle form. If this is accepted, then it is the space of a circle that should envelop the square frame. Examples of temple plan with a circular wall and a square *garbhagriha* have been found in Kerala. The circular plan was common to Buddhist monuments. But then the square as the fundamental principle gave rise to the square plan.

All the geometrical forms introduced in the building architecture—be it a house or temple—the most primary and most recommended form is square. Rectangular forms have to be evolved only after deciding the basic square, i.e. the square is extended rhythmically into a rectangle. There are two more geometrical patterns, namely, octagon and circle with their emanation from the square. These two are not recommended for a living space as it is a distortion of a square. These three patterns are linked to the experience of the inner being. When the inner space is in peace, the pattern of waves that appears in the inner space is said to be square. The square signifies *sattvaguna*. When the space is aroused to vibrate faster, the primal pattern of square turns into an octagon. This quality of space is called *rajasguna*. In the *Vastusastra*, these patterns carry certain technical names signifying the basic attributes of the Spirit. The square is called *nagara*, the octagon *dravida* and the circle, *vesara* with *sattva*, *rajas* and *tamas gunas*, respectively.

In the making of *mahavedi* and the fire altars of a Vedic *yajna*, the prescribed shapes are the rectangular, the triangular or the square. Circular and semicircular altars are also used in some cases. The dance styles follow the same ideational background. Bharatnatyam is a series of triangles in space; Kathakali, a square; Manipuri, a spiral or intertwined serpent and Kathak, an axis. Orissa evolves its distinctive basic motif of the tribhanga which is also a symmetrical and geometrical figure from the raisakha sthana.

CONCEPTUAL FORMS

The *Upanisadas* describe the world of name and form emanating from the formless, the unmanifest, the absolute (*para*) Brahman. This idea of form leads to formal principles of the arts. If forms are the visible extension or reflection of the one formless, then all objects, subtle and gross, are aspects of the reality. Hindu iconography follows this principle in creating the image of a deity.

In creating its identity, an image emerges as image twice: first in the sense of materializing the deity is reflection (image) and secondly in the sense of incorporating the transcendental suggestion based on proof. The idea-image integration seems to exist here in terms of manifesting the unmanifestable in the manner of ideal form because *rupa* signifies conceptual form and abides in the gross merely as reflection of something beyond and above. The concept of image involves not only the ideal form, i.e. deity, but also the latter's latent power and the form of its concretization. The deity reflected image seems to be comprehended in terms of a subtle suggestion (e.g. *bhava, prakriti,* etc.). Form is regarded not the material but a conceptual form. As metaphorically stated, form is reflected in image as moon is reflected in water. The water-moon simile is comprehensive, for what is reflected in image is limitless and yet encompassing the Three worlds.

Chapter 3

The Nature of Sound

THE SUPREME SOUNDLESS

The mathematical sign we know as zero (*sunya*) assigns the subsuming concept, the lack of an object. It is a kind of meta-sign that refers to the true and natural beginning. Metaphysically speaking, *sunya* is the ultimate reality. The Vedic seers have described the absolute void as Brahman, the first inconceivable thing in thought. The Brahman sets the stage for emergence of a self-conscious image. It refers to anything about which one may think. It can be grasped by negation as well as by affirmation in such categories of thought as 'full-and-empty' and 'with-and-without'. Seen in this way that which provides pre-existing reference to sound is 'soundless'. Several *Upanisadas* endeavour in various ways to explain the meta-sign:

There are two Brahmans to be contemplated: Brahman as sound and the soundless Brahman. Now it is by sound that the soundless is revealed. The sound here is *Om*. By the sound *Om* one proceeds upward and attains rest in the soundless. This is the goal, this is immortality, this is union and this is happiness. Just as a spider that climbs up its own thread reaches free space, so also one who meditates rises by saying *Om* and reaches ultimate freedom. But those who believe in Brahman as sound proceed differently. They listen to the sound within the space of the heart by placing the thumb on the ear. This is comprehended to seven things: a river, bells ringing, a copper vessel being struck, the creaking of a wheel, frogs, rain and speaking in a quiet place. Having transcended all characterization, (these sounds) merge into the supreme soundless, unmanifest Brahman. There, they are free from individualizing characters and differentiations, just as different sorts of nectar, having blended into honey, have lost their individualizing characters.

— *Maitri Upanisada*, VI.22

Thus, 'soundless' is the supreme reality conceived within the Universe of Brahman. The difference between sound and soundless is stated further: Brahman is that which cannot be heard by the ear but that by which the ear has hearing. The realization of soundless Brahman leads to immortality, that is, the one who comprehends this complexity immortalized in the concept:

When one has realized that which is soundless,
intangible, formless, unchanging, tasteless,
odourless, unwavering, beginningless and endless.
that which is infinite and perfectly stable,
then one is freed from the jaws of death.

— *Katha Upanisada* III, 15

Many primal myths around the world describe the beginning of creation from immobility and silence in the darkness. The beginning is an effect and for that reason is transient; it will go back to the state from which it has originated—as does Earth. That which is soundless has no beginning, no end and no effect. To describe the 'eternal', '*real* real', 'soundless', 'formless', 'endless', the ancients have used the word *neti neti,* not this, not this; i.e. beyond comprehension.

THE SOUL OF SOUND

The tenor of the *upanisadic* contemplation is to reduce the reality to the 'word-and-world principle'. All that is sound is Word. *Om* is the first word, the first symbol of the Universe. It is the Word before the world. It is the Word according to which the world is formed. It is first manifestation, the concentrated reality made word: sound, content, form, matter and spirit. *Om* is *sabdabrahman*, the self-affirmation of Brahman, the primeval sound of creation. The *upanisadic* sages have considered *Om* superior to the three Vedas, the immortal refuge:

Verily, when one finishes a Ric, he sounds out *Om*; similarly a Saman; similarly a Yajus. This sound is that syllable (*akshara,* imperishable). It is immortal, fearless. By taking refuge in it the Gods became immortal.

He who pronounces the syllable, knowing it thus, takes refuge in that syllable, in the immortal, fearless sound. Since the Gods became immortal by taking refuge in it, therefore he becomes immortal.

—*Chandogya Upanisada* 1.4.4-5

The spheroid (*brahmanda*) is pervaded as sound (*dhvani*). The sound called *nada* is the original vibration in the emanation of the Word. The concept of *nada* is related to *bindu* (drop, dot, spot); *bindu* is related to *beeja* (seed), the subtlest element of the Word and the cause of the unfolding of the Universe. The *Upanisadas* introduce the conception of sound in a remarkable way:

Just as when drum is beaten, one cannot take hold of the external sounds, but when taking hold of the drum or of the drumbeater, one takes hold of the sound also.

—*Brihadaranyaka Upanisada* II, 4,7-9

Sound is the primal imagery of the First Being. The Australian aboriginal myth provides a description: In the beginning there was nothing but waterholes, lumps of primal soups—soundless, sightless, unbreathing, unaware and unsleeping—each containing the essence of life. On the first morning the prehuman ancestral beings came out of the waterholes and, like the baby's cry, each opened his mouth and called 'I am', 'I am' And this first sound 'I am' was held as the most secret and sacred couplet of the ancestors' song. The ancestors sang their way all over the world. They wrapped the whole world in a web of song.

The *Atharvaveda* (IV.I) says that the Word was first born as the symbol of origins. According to the Jewish Christian tradition, in the beginning was the Word and the Word was with God and the Word was God. The Dogon of Africa envisaged creation in several stages each culminating in a sacred Word. All these traditions refer to the vibration of the cosmic sound of origin.

What is the connection between the *upanisadic* and the primal myths about the sound system? The answer is: a universal experience of the reality expressed in various ways—natural beginning from void, from soundless sound, world from word, vital sound emerging into a unity and so on.

THE ORGANIC SOURCES OF SOUND

Each of the Five Elements—Sky, Air, Fire, Water, Earth—has its own character and property, as alluded to in Chapter 2. When it is said that Elements combine in various proportions, it means their characters and properties merge together. For instance, sound is the physical property not only of the Sky but of the other four Elements as well:

Sky — Sound
Air — Sound, Touch
Fire — Sound, Touch, Vision
Water — Sound, Touch, Vision, Taste
Earth — Sound, Touch, Vision, Taste, Smell

Thus, sound is the physical property of all the Five Elements and it is the Earth Element alone in which all the physical properties combine. The basic rules are the same for all the other characters and properties. More esoterically, it is the sound system that makes life communicable. Since the Sky is eternal, sound is also eternal. All beings originate from sound and return to sound. If this theory of the Sacred Science is accepted, then it follows that life exists everywhere in the Universe. The sound system (the Sky Element) works beyond the solar system (the Fire Element).

All contingent beings—men, animals, birds, insects—are attuned to sound. The ear is the source of hearing sound and throat the source of producing sound. The organic pattern of sound is complex. There are five power centres in the human body which are awakened for hearing sound:

Forehead	—	Sky (illuminated *nada*)
Throat	—	Air (utterance of sound)
Heart	—	Fire (solar energy)
Genitals	—	Water (lunar energy)
Feet	—	Earth (ground of being)

When physical properties of body and sense organs combine with the Five Elements, the mediator awakens to the sound that pervades the Universe, proceeds upward by the sound *Om* and attains rest in the soundless.

All primal Elements have the physical property of sound and hence any part of the body can be the organic source of hearing and producing sound. Little wonder, therefore, that 'one listens to the sound within the space of the heart'. Or 'one hears without the ear'. In Sanskrit, one of the several names of snake is *cakchukasrava*, the 'one who hears with the eyes'.

THE SOUND OF NATURE

Of the natural sound, voices of the sea are mentioned in a vast maritime literature of East and West. Voices of the waterfalls and swirling rivers speak their own languages. Voices of the wind, like the sea, have an infinite number of vocal variations. The sounds of a tree falling in the woods is like a hurricane, a wolf, a cuckoo and anything one wishes to compare it with.

The bird-song, the sound of water creatures and the sound of terrestrial animal are the sounds of life. The language and songs of the birds have been a subject of much study. The vocalization of birds has often been studied in musical terms. Ornithologists have classified the types and functions of bird-song. Basically these are distinguished as follows: pleasure calls, distress calls, territorial defence calls, alarm calls, flight calls, nest calls and feeding calls.

Among the insects, the sound of the mosquito, the fly and the wasp are easily distinguishable. The beekeepers know how to distinguish all the variants of the bee-sound. Among the loudest of insects are the cicadas.

The sounds of water creatures are bewilderingly complex. While many fish have no sound-producing mechanism and no developed organs to hear sounds, many do produce unique sounds and some of these are very loud. In the early spring, marshes in many parts of the world are filled with the sounds of frogs and toads.

Among animals, the carnivores produce the greatest range of individual sounds. Many of these sounds such as the roaring of lions, the howling of wolves or the laughing of hyenas, have such striking qualities that they impress themselves instantaneously on the human imagination. The sounds made by primates have great diversity, varying from whistling, screaming and chattering to grunting and roaring. Man has numerous words to describe the animal sounds which are nearest to him. These are verbs, action words and most of them are onomatopoeic still: a dog *barks,* a puppy *yelps*, a cat *meows* and *purrs*, a cow *moos*, a lion *roars*, a goat *bleats*, a tiger *snarls*, a wolf *howls*, a mouse *squeaks*, a donkey *brays*, a pig *grunts* or *squeals*, a horse *whinnies* or *neighs*. The English language reproduces only those animals with which the Englishman has found himself in closest contact.

SOUND CONTEXTS

The voice is the primal instrument of communication. The non-human voice is either hallowed or feared. The scriptures speak of *akashavani,* the voice of the sky, which is often associated with prophetic messages. Some birds and animals are named by the peculiarity of their voice, i.e. the eternal naming of the sound. The *papiha* bird cries *pia-pia-pia-pia*; it is a message of love. At midnight, the bird *titahari* cries *tit-tit-tit-tit*; it is a signal for famine. If the cock's call is heard in the midnight, before the rising of the sun, it is considered inauspicious. Generally, a jackal makes its call *hue-hukke, hue-hukke* at night. If the call is *bheu-bheu* it is inauspicious. If a vulture or kite cries hovering over the village, it is an indication of some disease entering the village.

Voices of animals and birds are related in solar and cosmic radiation. The tribes of North-East India have many stories about birds. One such story refers to the relations of birds with the Sun and Moon: Once Doini, the Sun and Pollo, the Moon, did not appear for a long time and everything was dark. So the cock went to the home of the Sun and Moon and cried *ko-ko-ko-ko* and after some time the Sun came out of his house. Hence whenever it crows the Sun comes up into the sky.The Australian aborigines also speak of how the Sun was made to rise. It is by the laughter of *go-goor-gaga*, the laughing jackals, ringing through the air, that saved the light for the world. He laughs his loudest every dawn of day and awakens all sleepers before sunrise.

There are hard sounds like that of thundercloud and soft sounds like that of humming bees. Sound frequencies generated by some animals have been reported:

Animal	*Generated Sound*
Fruit-fly	225-575 hertz
Cricket	up to 5,000 hertz
Frogs	1,800-2,100 hertz
Toads	600-5,200 hertz
Newts	1,500-8,000 hertz
Birds	Average 6,000-10,000 hertz
Mammals	3,000-20,000 hertz

Listening, hearing and comprehending are three different processes. One may listen to or hear a sound but not necessarily recognize or comprehend it. Cognition is culture-specific. Comprehension of sound runs deeper than mere hearing or listening. Certain forms of sound such as the hooting of an owl and the cry of a dog or a jackal are considered inauspicious. Certain other forms such as *ulu-dhvani* (prevalent in Bengal), produced by twisting the tongue, the human imitation of the babbling of a he-goat and sounds of a conch-shell, drums and gongs, bells and cymbals are auspicious for the Hindus but not for the Muslims.

The physical emission of sound is a reflection of an inner spiritual reality. The internal unstruck sound is free from individualizing characters and differentiation. What our ears are hearing is the external struck sound classified variously in various traditions. A distinction is drawn between the physical and metaphysical sounds. Sounds of nature include not only those arising from the exterior physical world but also from the interior body complexity of humans, animals, birds and insects. The laws of nature apply to both. In yet another expression, sound is not a property of physics. The inward cognition of 'Krishna's flute' is an example of metaphysical sound. Here no flute is played but the inspired sound of the divinity is generated and heard by the meditator. This is proved by *real* self-experience and not by the theories of physics. The value of metaphysical sound lies in that it links the physical with the spiritual.

There is a Chinese proverb—'The five sounds make people deaf and the five colours make people blind'. There are two levels of sound in Chinese tradition: at the lower level, there is the natural, innocent, ordinary and unsung sound; at the higher level there is the hallowed, organized and manipulated sound. The ordinary unsung sound is called *sheng*, while *yin* is the high hallowed sound. The Chinese concept of sound is just like the Sanskrit word *atman* which connotes both the lowly self and the holy self. The unsung sound *sheng* is transformed into the hallowed sound *yin*, i.e. music and poetry. The *yin* becomes a corner of moral values. These terms have gathered rich cultural deposit along the course of historical evolution. In the first place, *sheng* and *yin* are two sides of the same coin. However, they have established a kind of division of labour. While the human voice can be described as both *sheng* and *yin*, the sound made by a non-humans is generally *sheng*, not *yin*. There is a host of human sounds like *jiaosheng* and *hansheng* for shouting, *husheng* for appeal, *xiaosheng* for laughter, *kusheng* for weeping, *tansheng* for sigh, *hansheng* for snoring, *naosheng* for quarrel and *shasheng* for war-cry, in which the usage of *yin* cannot find place. Also, *yin* is not used for the sound of door-knocking, rain, wind, machine, footsteps, etc.—only *sheng* is used. All this means that *yin* is not used to qualify sound at a particular level, particularly the base level. However, in modern Chinese, the bi-syllabic word *shengyin* is used for sound and thus the said division of labour disappears in this compound word.

CHAOTIC SOUND

In modern science, the Big Bang is associated with the theory of expanding Universe. The original lump of matter was located somewhere in a pre-existing void; fragments of the 'primeval egg' blown apart in the Big Bang. This notion is rejected on the ground that space itself and time were created, like matter, in the Big Bang; there was no 'outside' into which the explosion occurred. However, the Big Bang postulates a phase of turbulent energy prior to the appearance of matter and life.

The Sacred Science theories of 'expanding Brahman', the force of the infinitesimally small and infinitely dense *nadabindu*, *hiranyagarbha* and *sabdabrahman*, are close to modern science. But their difference is equally remarkable. The Big Bang acknowledges only physical forces. The *nadabrahman*, which attributes consciousness to creation-sound like the humming of black bees, the Australian aboriginal notion of 'creation-sound' comparable to the 'baby's cry'and prehuman ancestors 'singing the world into existence' are again very different from what the Big Bang suggests.

Chaotic sounds of thundercloud, earthquake and other natural phenomena are associated with the idea of cosmic disorder comparable to social disorder (arising from transgression of marriage rules, fighting, causing injustice, destruction of life, etc.). Celestial and earthly beings are considered to have physical and spiritual dimensions that are symbolically reflected in one another. Thunder and lightning are seen as the life-destroying radiation of the sky. Tribes of India perceive them as 'shouts in fear', 'loud noise in anger', '*ting tang* noise of war-dance', '*heen-heen-heen* sound of weeping', 'sound of war drums', 'loud gruntle of the fighting cloud-pigs' and so on. Earthquake is attributed to 'deep breaths of a great body', 'shout in fear crying', 'trembles at the impact of the mighty conflicts', 'shaking in anger', 'knocking', 'bumping' and all that create imbalance and gives an appropriate sense of doom.

In Hindu cosmology, the *tandava* form of dance marks the metaphysical level of dissolution of the world. The sound of Shiva's *damaru* and the movement of his dancing feet re-sculpture the tribal imagery of thunder and earthquake as signs of cosmic disorder.

SOUND AS MEASURE

Sound as space-measure is explicit in the *agamic* tradition. All the Five Elements are considered as space, a paradigmatic model of which is enshrined in South India, as shown in Chapter 2. With correspondence between the Elements and the divinity, one can draw the conclusion that sound qualifies and measures the sacred geography.

Space is impregnated with sound or sound particles called *nadabindu*. The totality of sound particles is *sabdabrahman*. Sound travels in waves in ten directions like a *kadamba* flower that buds in all directions or what is called the *kadamba mukula-nyaya*. In the natural philosophy of Australian aborigines, the creation-ancestors are believed to have scattered a trail of words and musical notes along the lines of their footprints. Hence there are in the world 'song waves' or 'song tracks', all from the soundless void. The 'song tracks' determine and guide the physical, social and ceremonial journey of the tribe. Sound is the measure not only of physical space (land) but of a clan, kinship, marriage and all that relates to social space.

Sound as time-measure is well developed in music. In metaphysics it is perceived as 'breath of life'. In outer space, waves of sound are produced by movement of air. In the space within the body of a living being, sound waves are produced according to *pranavayu* (movements of the vital air) and by the process of inhalation and exhalation.

Sound as linguistic measure has been worked upon in a significant way. Sometimes a distinction is made between the articulate sound associated with gross matter and the sound sorted and extracted by the listener from the gross matter. The first is called *dhavani* and the second *sphota*. The *sphota* is an indivisible entity over *dhvanis* (sounds), which are many in number and are uttered by the speaker in a temporal sequence in order to manifest the *sphota*, the real expressive words.

SOUND AS RITUAL

The Vedic revelation tells us in innumerable texts that *vak* (word) is not just a man-made invention or a mere tool of communication. It is ultimately Brahman itself. The *mantra* is the primordial word; its conception as God is fully developed in the *tantric* tradition. A *mantra* is composed of letters. Letters and their combination as syllables and words are all forms of manifested *sabda*, that is, Brahman forms. They are each and all forms of the creative stress, as uttered by the mouth, heard by the ear and apprehended by the mind. The *mantra* is intoned in the proper way according to *varna* (letter) and *svra* (rhythm). The relations of *varna, nada, bindu,* vowel and consonant in *mantra* constitute the deity.

Dhavani (both human voice and mechanical sound) is another constituent of the ritual language. To please Shiva, the worshipper produces a peculiar sound by his mouth, '*bum bum buhu*', imitating the babbling of a he-goat. Shiva is pleased best by the sound of a *damru*, Vishnu by the sound of a conch shell and Shakti deities by drums and gongs. All these three are propitiated by bells and cymbals. No Hindu worship is complete without ringing the hand-bell. In all forms of chants and recitation, the critical aspect is sound. *Dhvani* is, therefore, a *mantric* sign.

In *tantric* rituals, the very basis of initiation is the suitability of a specific *bija* (mystic letters) or *mantra*, its composition and pronunciation (sound) in relation to the capability of the noviciate, his nature and make-up of his mind. The novice has to make up his body *mantramaya* (alive with *mantras*). Each *nyasa* (stage of initiation) consists of touching various parts of one's own body, from head to foot, with the muttering of *bijas* or *mantras*, alphabet associated with the *nakshatras* (signs of lunar zodiac), *rashis* (signs of solar zodiac), *yoginis* (female divinities), *pithas* (sound centres), etc. Symbolic reflections of the sound principle are represented in Shakti iconographic form. For example, in the *mundamala* (garland of fifty severed heads) on the body of Goddess Kali, each of fifty heads stands for an alphabet. Similarly the *akshamala* (rosary) held by several Goddesses also symbolizes the garland of letters. The term, *aksha,* itself indicates beads representing the fifty letters of Sanskritic alphabet from *a* to *ksa*. Another attribute, *pustaka* (manuscript) in the hands of Goddess Saraswati and Srikula symbolizes the knowledge, i.e. words codified. Other *ayudhas* like *ghanta* (bell), *sankha* (conch shell) and *vina* (a musical instrument) are symbols of *sabdabrahman.* On this account Goddess Matangi (who is conceived as a *vina* player) is called the mother of the music, the one who could be propitiated through music recitation.

Here importance has been given to letter because man experiences sound only through letters, words and sentences. The linguistic sound gets expressed in metrical language, in song and prose. The exalted music, *mantra* or chant, is the ritual language, the peal of being. The *mantra* is the highest reach of language which man does not speak but which speaks to man, the language of power (divine, spiritual). Even as the peal of being, it is recited in silence, in whisper or in song. The exalted *mantra* is aroused in the consciousness of the performer and the consciousness sustains itself by the *mantra.* At this stage of conditioning, the word does not remain the word and the sound does not remain the sound.

The chanting and recitation of *mantric* sign are widely known in ritualistic traditions. Among the Mezatec Indians of New Mexico, the essence of the *shamanistic* tradition lies in ritual language, the making of the word. In a healing ritual, the *shaman* (diviner) receives inner images and instantaneously emits the word for them. The healing power is directly related to the ability of his visionary words, which draw together that which has been pulled asunder. Their cosmological image of the 'word and world' relationship corresponds to the Sanskritic traditions, as stated earlier.

SOUND AND LIGHT

It is not without significance that the *Rigveda* opens with the invocation of Fire and its last *sukta* is also dedicated to Fire. Brahman is described as that which 'shines in yonder sun, in the moon, in fire and in lightning'. Brahman is 'flame without smoke'. 'Brahman is sound'. 'From the mouth the Word came out and from the Word, Fire'. Sound is the quality of space. Luminosity is also the quality of space. It is the combination of sound and light that transforms all matter into energy. The Vedic seers expressed this idea with poetic imagery: With banked-up clouds, rumblings of thunder, the roaring wind and lightning flashes. Parjanya, the personification of rain, quickens the earth with his seed. He is the bringer of fertility, life and growth.

Sound and light are inseparable, because both are the *vibhutis* of Brahman. In all forms of worship, it is essential to combine them for making a ritual act sacred-effective.

Tribal epistemology explains the physics of sound and light in terms of passion for union: 'sound is the roaring of a passionate male and light is the shining hairpin of a woman who refuses to concede and throws it in anger', or 'sound is the thunder of an angry husband and light is the body's beauty of a fleeing wife'. What these human metaphors suggest is not the inseparability of sound and light but the virtual unity of elemental properties. In other words, there is an inherent fuzziness in sound-and-light relationship, something like 'quantum uncertainty principle'.

SOUND AND TIME

The Sun and Moon, day and night, seasons and sound serve as natural clock. Rituals are associated with astral mythology and the time for ritual is determined by astrological clock. Time is divisible by Nature. The Sun and Moon are such a pair that brings the physical phenomenon of light. Both have received a special accent of holiness. When the Sun rises, it collects all living beings in its raise. Birds are the first to announce its arrival. For most traditional cultures, cock is the timekeeper.

For example, the Santhals still depend upon the biological clock, the cock. Normally the cock calls three times between midnight and sunrise. These are named: (a) *margan sim rak* (the great cock crow) which calls between 1 am and 3 am; this is called *margan* (great) because it is heard after a long gap of time when the Santhals sleep at night; (b) *hudin sim rak* (the small cock crow) is heard after 3 am, before dawn; it means small call because the same is heard after a short interval; and (c) *setak sim rak* (the morning cock crow) is heard just before the sunrise. Having heard the last call, the villagers understand that the Sun is to rise and they should get ready for daily work.

In African societies biological time plays a major part. The biological timekeeper has been man's first tutor in that it reveals to man the rhythms and, through such rhythms, the division of time, or in any case of a time which can be split up into units.

The Chinese character, *shihlu,* is the note corresponding to the month. The quality of energy varies with the season; it can be translated into musical terms. The air moving into the cavity of the Earth reveals a celestial note and gives forth an earthly sound. Seasons and music are different elements of a single reality.

Among the Algerian peasants there is a proverb which says, 'If it thunders in January, take up the flute and tambourine; if it thunders in February don't use up your fodder'. Such rhymed phrases and proverbs are anticipation of the future event.

To Indian peasants certain sounds of animals and birds indicate famine, death and disease. For them sound is itself not a sequence of time (that is, the present), but becomes prophetic of what follows it (the future time). There are taboos with regard to the making of certain sounds symbolizing inauspiciousness. Absence of sound (that is, silence) on a particular occasion assumes a positive role in the maintenance of the society.

In music, time designates the basic rhythmical patterns. A movement is said to be in six-eight time (6/8), having 6 eighth-notes (quavers) to the bar. So also common time (4/4), waltz time (3/4), march time (4/4 or 6/8) and free time, without any regular accent. The association of *ragas* with some particular seasons and timings had been a peculiar aspect of Indian music. For example, the *ragas* such as Bhairavi, Bhairav, Hindol, Jaunpuri, Todi and Bilawal are associated with morning; Sarang, Desi and Gunkali with noon; Bhimpalasi, Purya Dhanashri, Patdeep, Pilu and Multani with evening; and Purya, Kamaj, Suddha-Kalyan, Kamod, Shankara, Behag, Bhageshri, Molkouns and Darbari with night. There are also twilight *ragas* and midnight *ragas*. There is a feeling that these *ragas*, if sung specifically at the appropriate time to each, will have a special appeal on the listeners' minds. This system of associating *ragas* with particular timings was once prevalent in Persia, Iran and Iraq as well.

THE SOUND BEYOND

Indian classical music refers to *nada*, 'sound', *sruti*, 'microtones', *svara*, 'notes' and *tala*, 'metrical cycles'. A distinction has been made between the *anahat*, 'unstruck' and the *ahata*, 'struck' sound, the first being a vibration of ether, which cannot be perceived by men but is the basis of all manifestations. It forms permanent numerical patterns which are the basis of the world's existence. It is in the soundless Brahman, the *anahatnada*, 'unstruck sound', that Gods delight. Man cannot hear the celestial silence, but can discover its correspondence with *nadabrahman,* the sound Brahman', *sangitapurusa,* the 'music person' in the manifestation of sound through deities, colours, gems, time of day, seasons and psychic emotional states. The *Upanisadas* have spoken of sound as 'divine lute' and 'man-made lute'. The *Natyasastra* speaks of the 'bodily lute' and the 'wooden lute'. The Sufi tradition refers to human body as a flute. The sound is produced in the 'inner space', the *atman*, 'self'. From the all-pervasive void, the 'stressless silence', emerges *mulaspanda,* 'primeval heaving', i.e. original vibration giving rise to 'great sound', *Om*. The original unmanifested sound rests in a state of involution against the background of fundamental silence. From this primordial, transcendent state, it descends to the subtle, less subtle and the gross level wherein it becomes a physically audible phenomenon. Thus, silence can be heard. The *yogi* attains a state of liberation from the senses and he hears the *anahata,* the 'unstruck' sound.

This perception is close to the western concept of the Music of Spheres, which goes back to the Greeks, particularly the school of Pythagoras. Having discovered the mathematical correspondence between the ratios of the harmonics in a sounding string and noting that the planet and stars also appeared to move with perfect regularity, Pythagoras united discovery with intuition and conjectured that the two types of motion were both expressions of a perfect universal law, binding music and mathematics. Pythagoras is reported to have been able to hear the celestial music, though none of his disciples was able to do so. But the intuition persisted.

What comes out clearly from both Indian and Greek sources is, when silence is heard in the 'inner space', perfection is achieved, number becomes audible and luminosities in terms of sound appear.

Chapter 4

The Arena of Space

THE BODY OF THE UNIVERSE

Indian cosmology holds that the Universe is infinite and expanding beyond the arena of geometrical space where the drama of Nature is acted out. The Vedic hymns of the Golden Germ (*Hiranyagarbha*) and the Cosmic Person (*Purusa*) define the living body of the Universe in geometrical terms. The Golden Germ refers to the life-principle. The sacrifice of the Cosmic Person with thousand heads, thousand eyes and thousand feet signifies the infinite forms of matter—the Elements of the Earth and the Sky. The mystery of reality deepens: 'Encompassing the Earth all sides, He exceeded it by ten fingers breadth'. It means *Purusa* was more than a single individual and more than a sum of all individuals. The *upanisadic* sages introduced the conception of Brahman, which transcends geometry of surfaces. By infusing the image of *Purusa* into the conception of Brahman, the sages gave a new language more akin to physics than biology. They conceived a world of matter arising out of space and disappearing back into space, the ultimate ground of the world. The course of evolution from the primal *Atman,* through the Elements, is thus stated:

> From this Soul (*Atman*), space arose; from space, wind;
> from wind, fire; from fire, water; from water, the earth;
> from the earth, herbs; from herbs, food; from food; semen;
> from semen, the person.
>
> —*Taittiriya Upanisada* II, 1

This makes it possible to think of the interrelationship between the Soul and the Elements. The *Atman* is entering from a state of larger space to a smaller space. In other words, the *Atman* simultaneously exists in two widely separated spaces. The individual soul (*atman*) is identified with the infinite Great Soul (*parmatma*). The apparent paradox has been resolved by introducing the term Brahman, the expanding one:

What is called Brahman—that is the same as what the space outside of a person is. What the space outside of a person is—that is the same as what the space within a person is. What the space within a person is—that is the same as what the space here within the heart is. That is the Full, the unchanging.

—*Chandogya Upanisada III*, 12, 79

The *Upanisada* shows the ascending way to find the true perspective of space as a whole, the fundamental law of the Universe:

Space is greater than radiance, for in space are the sun and moon, lightning, the stars and fire. Through space one calls, through space one hears and through space one replies. In space one delights or one does not delight. In space one is born and onto space one is born. Meditate on space.

—*Chandogya Upanisada VII*, 12, 1

The Vedic revelation of the origin of the world from *Purusa* and the *upanisadic* conception of Brahman as the primal entity held out the promise of an explanation. Now, the two forms of Brahman upheld the totality of the Universe:

There are two forms of Brahman: the embodied and the bodiless, the mortal and the immortal, the stable and the moving and the tangible and the intangible.

The embodied is different from the air and from space; it is the mortal, the stable and the tangible. The essence of this embodied, mortal, stable and tangible one is that (sun) which gives heat, for it is the essence of the tangible.

The bodiless is air and space; it is the immortal, the moving and the intangible. The essence of the bodiless, immortal, moving and intangible one is the Person in the sphere of yonder sun, for he is the essence of the intangible. This is with relation to the cosmic powers.

Now with relation to the *atman:* The embodied one is what is different from the life breath and from the inner space within the heart. The mortal, the stable and the tangible one is the eye, for it is the essence of the tangible.

Now the bodiless is the life breath and the inner space within the heart. It is the immortal, the moving and the intangible. The essence of the bodiless, immortal, moving and intangible one is the Person in the right eye, for he is the essence of the intangible.

—*Brihadaranyaka Upanisada II*, 2.3, 1-5

Thus, the embodied Universe is real because it is the essence of the intangible and the bodiless Universe is the *real* of the real. The embodied Universe cannot be understood without a reference to the bodiless Universe which is the cause of everything. The mysterious presence of the bodiless space has been explained:

He who dwells in the space, yet is other than the space, whom the space does not know, whose body is the space, who controls the space from within—he is the *Atman* within you, the Inner Controller, the Immortal.

—*Brihadaranyaka Upanisada* III, 7.12

THE FOUR QUARTERS OF THE SKY

The Golden Germ splits into two halves. The process of auto-fission of the one creative principle into two is fundamental to the Vedic and *pauranic* cosmology. It is expressed in several ways—man and woman, Husband and Wife, Father and Mother, Heaven and Earth, the Upper and the Lower. This is further elaborated as the creation of the four. The four quarters of space, enclosing the Sky, form the world *swastika* of Brahma, the creator and Vishnu, the preserver. The bounded four regions (*disha*) have no intrinsic reality but by the movement of the sun they form a *swastika*. The union of the two principles is involved here, namely, the centre and the circumference. Each created object or organism has this essential character; it is its centre which expands into the circumference through the diameter. The measure of the centre with its diameter determines the expansive circle (*mandala*). The threefold concept has been the basis of the triadic creation of the Vedas:

1. Centre — *Yajurveda*
2. Diameter — *Rigveda*
3. Circumference — *Samveda*

In Indian cosmology the triad—the three kinds of knowledge, the three gods, the three life-principle, the three *gunas*, the three worlds and three fires—forms a pattern of the cosmos.

There is also a mention of the ten quarters of space typifying the principle of Sky which is the foremost material manifestation.

THE WORLDS OF ENDLESS SPACE

Modern cosmologists are of the opinion that about 100 billion stars, including the Sun, make up the Milky Way galaxy, a wheel-shaped structure. This galaxy is itself a part of a group of galaxies that form a cluster, while clusters in turn form the supercluster of many thousands of galaxies. Powerful telescopes reveal that this pattern of hierarchical clustering prevails throughout the cosmos. What binds the Universe together are the cosmic strings which are hypothesized to have some bizarre properties. Long long ago sage Yajnvalkya said to his disciple Aruni, 'This world and the next world and all beings and all natural phenomena are strung together by the thread, the Inner Controller, the Immortal, the Brahman'. Such knowledge of the Universe is based on the transcendental experience of the sages which led to the final revelation. What they remembered was what they actually saw in the vision. Revelation is a past recall and hence has a truth value.

Pauranic cosmology mentions the Golden Germ with its seven sheaths comprising of the Universe and the individual, mind and matter. The group of seven is given many epithets, the Seven Great Ones, which are inseparably joined and which possess the highest potential power for creating subsequent forms. The sevenfold scheme within the Egg is further elaborated by saying that the seven worlds, seven islands, seven seas and seven mountains lay in the Egg. The seven mountains are like the seven zones of a sphere (*mandala*). The whole system of stars, planets and constellations is conceived of a *chakra* rotating like a potter's wheel. The vast space is an ocean in which the stars are arranged like the body of a dinosaur or giant alligator. The imagery of the wheel implies a relatively fixed centre.

The Buddhist *Abhidharmakosha* describes the Universe as follows: A circle of wind floats in space. The wind circle is disk-shaped, 1,059 *yojanas* in circumference and 1,600,000 *yojanas* in depth (there are various explanations concerning the length of a *yojna*; one says it is about seven kilometres). Resting on the wind circle is a disk of water; it has a diameter of 1,203,450 *yojanas* and a depth of 800,000 *yojanas*. Above the water circle is a disk-shaped layer of golden earth of the same diameter and 320,000 *yojanas* in depth. Its upper surface supports mountains, seas and islands. The diameters of the water and golden earth layers are the same, because these two layers were originally a single layer, or more correctly a cylinder, of water only. There are nine mountain ranges on the surface of the golden earth layer. Towering in the very centre is Mount Sumeru, with seven ranges forming concentric squares around it. They are squares, with sides of 80,000 *yojanas*.

The *Bhagavata Purana* describes Meru Mountain and the planetary system known as Bhumandala, which is like a lotus flower and its seven islands are compared to the whorl of the lotus. The place known as Jambudvipa is in the middle of that whorl. In Jambudvipa there is a mountain named Sumeru, which is made of solid gold. The height of this mountain is 84,000 *yojanas*, of which 16,000 *yojanas* are below the earth. Its width is estimated to be 32,000 *yojanas* at its summit and 16,000 *yojanas* at its foot. This king of mountains, Sumeru, is the support of the planet earth. There is another mountain known as Lokaloka. The island of Plaksadvipa is twice as broad as

Jambudvipa. The island is divided into seven regions each with a mountain and a large river. The area beyond Lokaloka is called Aloka-varsa and beyond Aloka-varsa is the pure destination of persons who desire liberation. Vertically the Sun is situated just in the middle of the Universe, the space between Bhurloka and Bhuvarloka. The distance between the Sun and the circumference of Anda-golaka, the globe of the Universe, is estimated to be twenty-five *koti yojanas* (two billion miles). Because the Sun enters the Universe and divides the Sky, it is known as Martand. The Sun is not stationary; it is also moving like the other planets. The Sun's movements determine the duration of night and day. The Moon is situated 100,000 *yojanas* above the rays of the sunshine. Above the Moon by a distance of 200,000 *yojana*s are some stars and above these is the planet Venus. Above Venus by 200,000 *yojanas* is Mercury, above Mercury by 200,000 *yojanas* is Mars; above Mars by another 200,000 *yojanas* is Jupiter; and above Jupiter is the planet Saturn. These seven stars circumambulate Dhruvaloka; which is the residence of Lord Vishnu. It is situated 1,300,000 *yojanas* from the seven stars. In the planetary system of Dhruvaloka are the planets of the Fire God, Indra Prajapati, Kashyapa and Dharma. The Rahu is situated 10,000 *yojanas* below the Sun and Moon. Below Rahu by another 100,000 *yojanas* are the planets—Siddhas, Caranas and Vidyadharas and below these are planets such as Yakshaloka and Raksaloka. Below these planets is the Earth and 70,000 *yojanas* below the Earth are the lower planetary systems—Atal, Vital, Sutal, Talatal, Mahatal, Rasatala and Patal. Demons and rakshasas live in these lower planetary systems with their wives and children, always engaged in sense gratification and not fearing their next births. The sunshine does not reach these planets, but they are illuminated by jewels fixed upon the hoods of snakes. Because of these shining gems there is practically no darkness. Those living in these planets do not become old or diseased and they are not afraid of death from any cause but the time factor. There are also hellish planets to which a sinful man goes. Humans act differently and therefore they suffer different reaction. There are twenty-eight hells, each meant for different types of sins committed in a lifetime. Pious persons are elevated to the highest planetary system, where the demigods live. When the results of their pious activities are finished, they come back again to this Earth.

Traditional vision leaps into the anthropic principle to appreciate the infinite dimensions of the Universe. The expanse of the infinite Universe is beyond ordinary comprehension. The scriptures have given a classified description of places conceivable to man, the thinker. The location of the places has been measured in astronomical calculations given by the *Jyotir Veda*. The hundreds and thousands of places (stars, planets) are self-organised in the Universe of Brahman, each having an operating deity (the law) who follows the orders of the Supreme Person (God, Govinda or Krisna). This is what the material scientists call gravity or any such similar idea. The deities of the planets are persons and the Supreme power is also a person. Thus, the living Universe is moving and unmoving. The Supreme Person controls all and contains all. As Krisna says—

> O Son of Kunti, it is solely My impregnating presence that cause Mother Nature to give birth to the animate and inanimate. Because of Me (through *Prakriti*) the worlds revolve in alternating cycles (of creation and dissolution).
>
> —*Bhagvad Gita* IX.10

> O Arjuna, the Lord is lodged in the hearts of all creatures and by His cosmic delusion (*maya*) compels all beings to rotate as if attached to machine.
>
> —*Bhagvad Gita* XVIII.61

Lord Krisna while revealing His cosmic form (*Vishvarupa*) to Arjuna:

> Arjuna saw the multifarious marvellous presence of Deity—infinite in forms, shining in every direction of space, omnipotence all-pervading, adorned with countless celestial robes and garlands and ornaments, upraising heavenly weapons, fragrant with every lovely essence, His mouth and eyes everywhere!
>
> If a thousand suns appeared simultaneously in the sky, their light might dimly resemble the splendour of that Omnific Being!
>
> There, resting within the infinite Form of the God of gods, Arjuna beheld the entire Universe with all its diversified manifestations.
>
> —*Bhagvad Gita* XI. 10-13

The ordinary man's mind cannot see the 'body of the Universe'. Arjuna saw it through the astral eye of light. Such communication presupposes a spiritual 'voice', the sacred word or intuitive thought.

THE ARTICULATION OF SACRED SPACE

Man's position in the space is not something that can be detached from the reality. But his imaginal ability takes him far beyond the given space. He constructs two types of reality—mythical and mathematical. The mythical space is closely related to faith; the mathematical space is constructed on reason. Both are products of human consciousness and yet opposed to one another. Traditional thought brings the most diverse elements into a universal relation which is experience in life. The division of space into Heaven and

Earth is based on the distinction between content and position. Here the distinction between celestial and terrestrial, based on natural phenomena, is purely experiential. The physiological space differs from metric space, but the primary spatial difference is overcome by mythical configuration—cognition of 'sacred space'. The sacred geometry and the sacred number are the true basic phenomenon of the divine. The mythical and experiential space merge into a physical substance and a universal order is drawn upon.

The *upanisadic* sages had visualized the truth of unity of all experience and harmony of all existence. Since all things and beings originated from the one universal Self, they represent the same reality. Thus, in essence, the whole Earth is sacred and so also all beings and things of the world. Of them some are more sacred and effective than others and hence fit for ritual performances. Four terms have been used to describe the forms of 'sacred space'.

KSETRA

The Sanskrit word *Ksetra* (Pali, *khetta*), with a particular degree of generality, refers to physical space of all types: field, landed property, enclosed spot or ground, portion of space, place of origin, dominion, region, etc. The core meaning of the word is extended to a conglomerate of wide-ranging aspects, from geometric forms to metaphysical expressions—plane figure as triangle, circuit, superficies, house, town, seat, sphere of activity, source, extent, wife, womb, body, primeval soul or matter. The total field of spatial meaning is transformed when used in spiritual contents. A core identification of meaning can be sought in a set of four generalizing expressions: a perceptual distinctive unit of physical space such as field and plough land, a model characterized by geometric form such as diagram for an image panel, a biological category indicating generative process such as woman and a conceptual construct of body and/or mind as a spiritual sphere such as body and the knower of the body that is, Self. As a categorical term, *ksetra* reflects various layers of conceptual thinking : Physical/Metaphysical—stands for both body and mind; Mathematical/Mythical—refers to spatial phenomenon measured and drawn up in relation of forms such as a perfect geometric form called *rupaksetra,* 'the cosmic image panel'; Inner/Outer—the body is called *ksetra* and the soul that dwells in the body is *ksetrajna;* Macrocosm/Microcosm—the whole earth is *ksetra* and the position of stars in the sky is also *ksetra.* The *tirtha-ksetra*, a place of pilgrimage on Earth, is conceptualized as a microcosm. All sacred places are not *ksetra.* Only a cluster of special places of pilgrimage is given the categorical term tirtha-*ksetra*. Kashi (Varanasi or Benaras), Kamarupa in Assam, Purusottam (Puri), Gaya, Prayaga (Allahabad) are *siddhaksetra*, the place of supreme attainment. Kuruksetra, Kedarksetra, Varahmula, Gajaksetra and Pundarikaksetra are meritorious places. There are other places of supreme importance. Kuruksetra is sacred to Brahma and hence also called Brahmaksetra. Puri is sacred to Vishnu. Bhuvaneswar is sacred to Shiva. Jajapur in Orissa is sacred to the Goddess Parvati. The *ksetras* are listed in the *Mahabharata* and several of the eighteen *Puranas*. Everything of the cosmos that is considered powerful and auspicious finds a place in them. The notion of *ksetra* is found also in the Jain and Buddhist traditions. The Jain places of pilgrimage are of two classes—one is *siddhaksetra*, the places where holy men have attained *nirvana* and the other *atisayaksetra*, the places which have assumed importance because of temples, idols, or occurrence of certain miraculous events. The Buddhist scriptures mention *buddhaksetra*, the Buddha-field, region or, usually, world or world system in which a particular Buddha lives and operates. The *upaksetra* or subordinate Buddha-field has been stated to be four times the size of a *buddhaksetra*.

Mandala

Larger than the *ksetra* is *mandala*. The tantric Buddhist literature describes the ordering of *mandala* by means of which a pupil is consecrated. It is inscribed in a spot or in a house as *tantric* drawings of small size, generally three cubits plus three inches, using the sacred writing colours or powder made from the five gems or the grains of rice. The esoteric *mandalas* are the geometric representations showing the Buddha's manifold far-reaching presence. The Buddha pervades the Universe.

Pitha

The term *pitha* is used for places, 'benches' or 'seats' of the Goddesses. Each of these seats is considered as a manifestation of the 'female power'. *Tantric* Buddhist also refers to *pitha* and *upa-pitha*. The *pithas* are Jalandhara, Orddiyana, Purnagiri and Kamarupa; the *upa-pithas* are Malava, Sindhu and Nagara. There are other kinds of sacred territories associated with Buddhism. The four cardinal centres of the Hindu ascetic organization, established by the Ádi Shankaracharya and located in the four corners of India, are Jyotismath in the north (Himalaya), Puri in the east (coast), Sringeri in the south and Dwarka in the west (coast). They are also called *pitha*.

Tirtha

The Sanskrit term *tirtha* applies to all things held to be sacred and pure. As a conceptual category it exists in various forms such as speech, water, land, body, limbs, time, trees, places resorted to by Gods and so on. The feet of a Brahmana, the back of a cow, the limb of one's own wife, one's own eyes and the right ear are *tirthas*. The part of the little finger of a twice-born is called *tirtha* sacred to Prajapati; the part of the root of the thumb is called *tirtha* sacred to Brahma; the part of the top of the thumb is called *tirtha* sacred to Gods; and the part of the root of the forefinger is called *tirtha* sacred to the manes. Places where fire sacrifice and ancestral rites are performed, a temple or a house where the Veda is being studied, a cow-pen, a park or a place where a *soma* drinker dwells, a place where the banyan tree exists, a place where the *Purana* is being recited, or where one's teacher stands, or where a chaste housewife dwells, or where a father and a worthy son dwell are *tirthas*. Sanctity is caused to a place by the presence of lotus plants, basil plants and wood-apple trees. Water is considered as a potent agent in the removal of sin. Holy or consecrated water is *tirtha*. Particular sanctity is attached to river fords, certain divine waters, mountains and forests. The Buddhist *tirthas* are the places associated with the life of the Buddha. In the Jain scriptures, the *jin-sasana* or *dharma* itself is the *tirtha*. The one who creates *tirtha* is *Tirthankara*. Following on the *Brahma Purana*, the number of *tirthas* is so large that they cannot be enumerated even in hundreds of years. The *Vayu Purana* declares that there are three-and-a-half crores of *tirthas* on earth, in the sky and in the aerial region, all of which have their abode in River Ganga. There are three classes of *tirthas:* (1) *Manastirthas:* such as truth, compassion and self-restraint; (2) *Jangam tirthas*: such as the virtuous ones, parents, preceptors, husband and wife; and (3) *Sthavara tirthas*: such as the ten types of places of pilgrimage—created by god; associated with demon; established by the sages; created by the kings; located in the four corners of India; the seven places (*saptapuri*) bestowing liberation; the twelve shafts of light (*jyotirlinga*); the self-manifest (*svayambhu linga*); a cluster of seven seas, seven forests and seven mountains; places fit for ancestral rites; places possessing the mutilated limbs of Goddess Sati; and places of supreme attainment (*mokshatirtha*). Some places have acquired such great importance that others are named after them. There are five Prayaga in the Himalaya, each at the confluence of two rivers; five rivers, each called Ganga; and seven mouths of the River Godavari, sacred to seven sages. *Pauranic* description in respect of *tirthas* is graphic and complete, giving such details as the total area, the location of shrines, boundaries, etc. The *Prayaga-Mandal* is five *yojana* in circumference. The Kashi-*ksetra* is of two *yojana*-and-a-half east and west and half a *yojana* broad north and south; out of this Varanasi extends up to the River Asi in the south and Varuna in the north. Many *tirthas* are named in one place. Thirty-three crores of *tirthas* are located in Kashi. Each *tirtha* has a presiding God or Goddess. In some cases, more than one God may hold equal importance. Kashi is *Shiva-ksetra*; also *Vishnu-ksetra*, because here Vishnu assumes the epithet of Keshava.

PATTERNS IN SOCIAL SPACE

From the point of view of the physical form, there are four types of Indian villages: (1) 'shapeless cluster' or agglomerate with streets not forming an integral part of design; (2) 'linear cluster' or rows of houses; (3) 'square or rectangular cluster' or agglomerate with straight streets running parallel or at right angles to one another; and (4) 'isolated homestead', that is, a number of houses treated together as a unit.

Ecological factors seem to be responsible for various types of human settlements. Social and cultural considerations are also equally important. In the eastern coastal tract, the 'linear settlement' and 'close housing' are possible only because of class solidarity. In the middle Gangetic river valley, compact settlements are formed for reasons of defence. Social geometry draws upon the village landscape. Each of the four castes of men (*varna*) is assigned one of the four sides—the Brahmana in the north, the Ksatriya in the east, the Vaishya in the south and the Shudra in the west.

Generally the house faces eastward in order to get the morning Sun, or westward to attract more fresh air. Ecological explanations apart, in South India houses generally face either east or north, because in people's perception, the southern direction is dominated by the God of Death and the west by that of darkness.

The house pattern and the use of space coincide very closely with social concern, particularly regarding the form of the house and the functional use to which various parts are put. In South India, the granaries of all the people of a village are located at a distance from the main settlement for protecting the food reserve from fire. In Central India, the grain-bins are kept generally in the anterior portion of the house. Special privileges are, sometimes, assigned to the use of a certain portion of the building. In Manipur, the dwelling is so arranged that on the verandah, near the wall, there is seat of honour and rooms are reserved for the head of the family and the eldest son. In South

India and elsewhere, places are allocated for the household God, or for the menstruating women, childbirth, marriage, etc.

CANONS OF RITUAL SPACE

In Hindu perception, the whole earth is sacred, though some places are more sacred-effective and powerful than others. The Mahadaniya villages of the Oraon in Jharkhand have acquired special sanctity. As the legend has it: Once upon a time, a huntsman shot the sparrow and away flew the bird. Its blood fell in different villages of the country. The village in which the sparrow's head fell, became 'sacred of the first order' and those in which the blood from its wings fell became 'sacred of the second order'. Once every nine or ten or twelve years, the spirit of the sparrow is propitiated in these villages. The sacrifice of a buffalow or a cow or a sheep or a fowl is offered for the general well-being of the community.

Functionally, all the sacred-effective spaces can be classified into 'purity space' and 'protection space'. A 'purity space' is that which purifies the body of a man and makes him fit for liberation. Such are the temples and other shrines of God. The effectiveness of a 'purity space' lasts only so long as it remains free from physical or moral pollution. The scriptures have laid down elaborate rules for maintaining the sacred character of a place, as also of a person or an object. A 'protection space' is that where one is protected from the incursion of the evil from outside. As mentioned in the *Ramayana:* Lakshmana made a 'protection space' for Sita; and no sooner had Sita transgressed it than she fell a victim of evil Ravana. The diviner, in many parts of India, draws a circle about his place, chanting appropriate *mantras*. That prevents the evil from causing any harm or hindrance to the performer and the performance. Such a place is called *gahabar,* a Sanskrit word for cave. The nuptial room called *kohbar,* where the newly-wed couple perform the fertility rite, is also made a 'protection space'.

The Hindu sacred space has a vision. The kitchen of a Brahmana household is not merely a cooking place but a *sanctum sanctorum.* In one corner of the room, generally in the south-eastern direction, a raised square platform serves as altar for the family deity. The inner courtyard, rectangular in shape, has a mound reserved for the holy basil plants and a flag-pole hoisting the insignia of Hanumana, the Monkey God, is right there. In the outer courtyard, some families may enshrine ancestral spirits and minor deities. Depending on its size and composition, every village has a shrine. On the boundary of the village, a triangular or a pyramid-shaped mound represents the Mother Earth, the guardian deity of all the villagers, regardless of their social and religious denominations. Crossing the threshold of his house, a villager moves into larger and larger spaces through the centres and networks of ritual.

A study of the cosmic geometry of Vijayanagar in South India has demonstrated how a *mandala* is a major regulating model for royal Hindu cities. Patterns in space and time acquire meaning and power through geometric similarity and synchronized parallelism to cosmic shapes and astronomical cycles.

THE COSMIC PLAY

The organizing principle of space gets crystallized in the sacred geometry (Fig.5). There appears a circle with 360° in circumference. The centre is a dimensionless point symbolizing the expanding Brahman. The dotted circle is the point expanded. Within the circle, the cosmos appears as *swastika* with four angles of 90° each, forming a square which signifies the four-faced Brahma, the creator. The Three lines come together to form a cosmic triangle, representing the first threes: three forms of life (God, Animal and Man), three worlds (earth, middle region and heaven), three Gods (creator, preserver and destroyer), three microcosmic-macrocosmic properties (light, energy and inertness), three principles of life (assimilation – elimination, growth and procreation), three aspects of time (past, present and future), three *vidyas* (*Yajurveda, Rigveda and Samveda*) and similar other triads. This self-organized Universe of Brahman is the theatre of the Cosmic Play.

For a religious man, the Cosmic Law has the highest ethical values. The cosmic episodes are remembered at a higher metaphysical level and dramatized in a ritual way. This binds the human being to a shared level of understanding. The entirety of the Cosmic Play repeats in human life and ceremonies. Applying the sacred history, one can explain the meaning of symbolic performances.

The *Rigveda* reveals : 'In the beginning darkness was wrapped around by darkness'. At that state arose *Hiranyagarbha*, the sustainer of the Earth and Heaven. He bestowed life-force and hardy vigour to the actors of the world-order. The sacred city of Kashi, a Sanskrit word for luminous space, symbolizes *Hiranyagarbha* and serves as the paradigmatic theatre of the cosmos. It is represented by a holy circle, a quadrangle, a conch shell and the image of Shiva (Fig.6), signifying the Universe. Here the circle symbolizes the cosmic space, the quadrangle symbolizes the cosmic time, the conch symbolizes the life-principle and the anthropomorphic image symbolizes the universal Self.

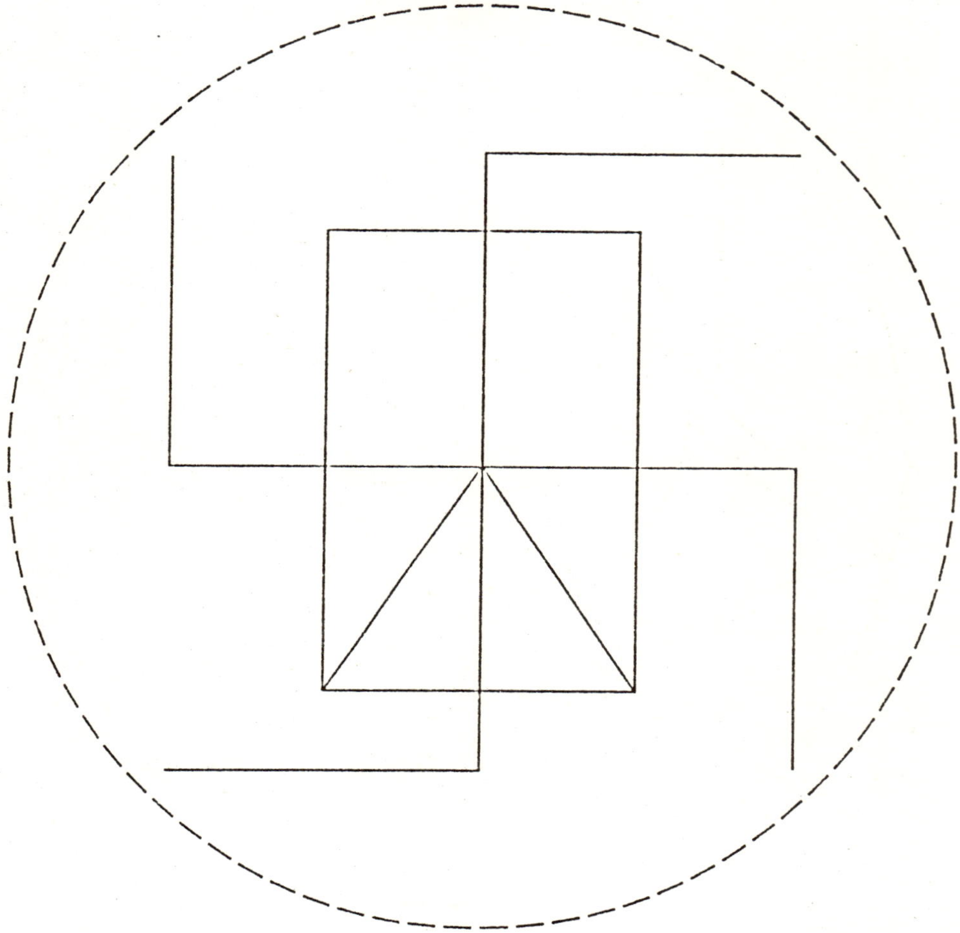

Fig. 5. The Universe of Brahman

Kashi is conceptualized in the mathematical arrays. The *ksetra* is situated on Shiva's trident at the centre of space and time. Its cosmological structure, marked by a holy circuit in the radius of five *kosa*, represents the five fundamental configurations—five sheaths or envelops (the food sheath, the vital sheath, the psychic sheath, the knowledge sheath, the blissful sheath) and five materiality (earth, water, fire, air, sky). Kashi's three segments signify the totality of the Universe. Kashi is a place where earthly dissolution is overcome and all beings rest here for ever. This Kashi is an infinite void. The finite Kashi is *mahasmasana,* a great cremation ground. The inner complexity of the infinite Kashi is made simpler and comprehensible at the finite earthly

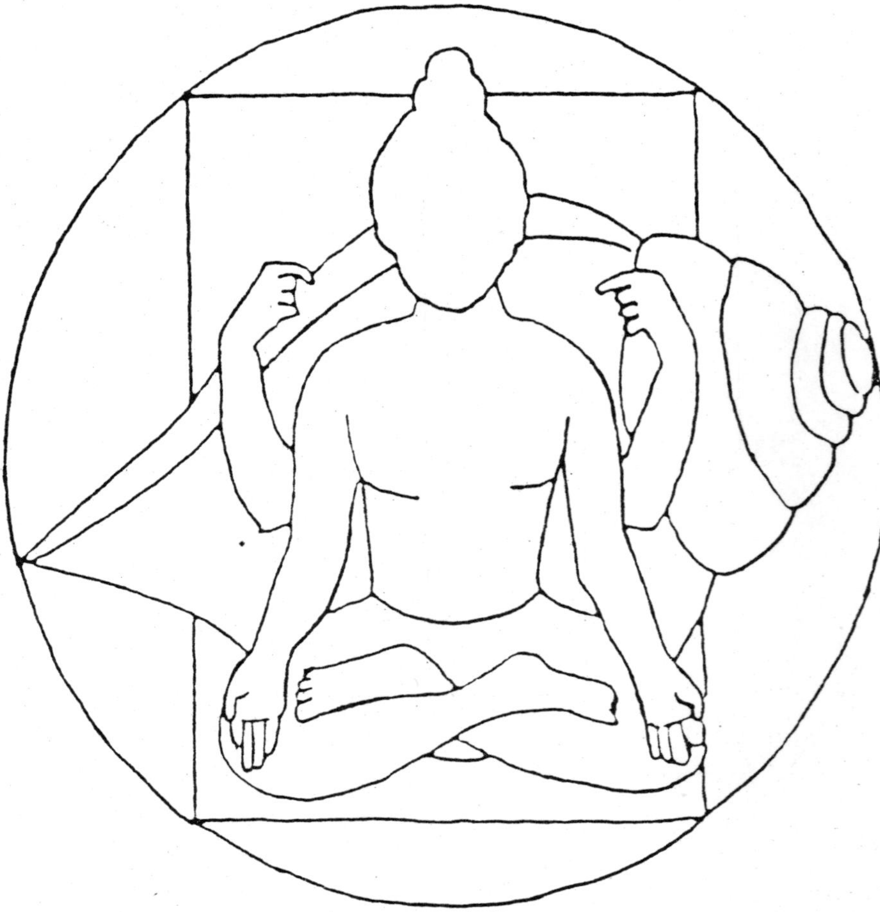

Fig. 6. The Cosmic Kashi-*ksetra*

Kashi, the divine theatre. The pilgrims echo the Cosmic Play. They move along the three concentric circles (Fig.7). The inner sanctum, formed by three sectors, represents the microcosm; the movement in the radius of five *kosa*, signifies the mesocosm; and the circumambulation in the radius of eighty-four *kosa* stands for the macrocosm where all the thirty-three crores of Gods and Goddesses reside. In this scheme of pilgrimage, one moves towards the full realization of the innermost spiritual experience.

One of the most important hymns of the *Rigveda* mentions the sacrifice of *Purusa*, the Cosmic Person. This sacrifice made the principle of sacrifice itself, that is, it made the world sacred by creating out of the process of

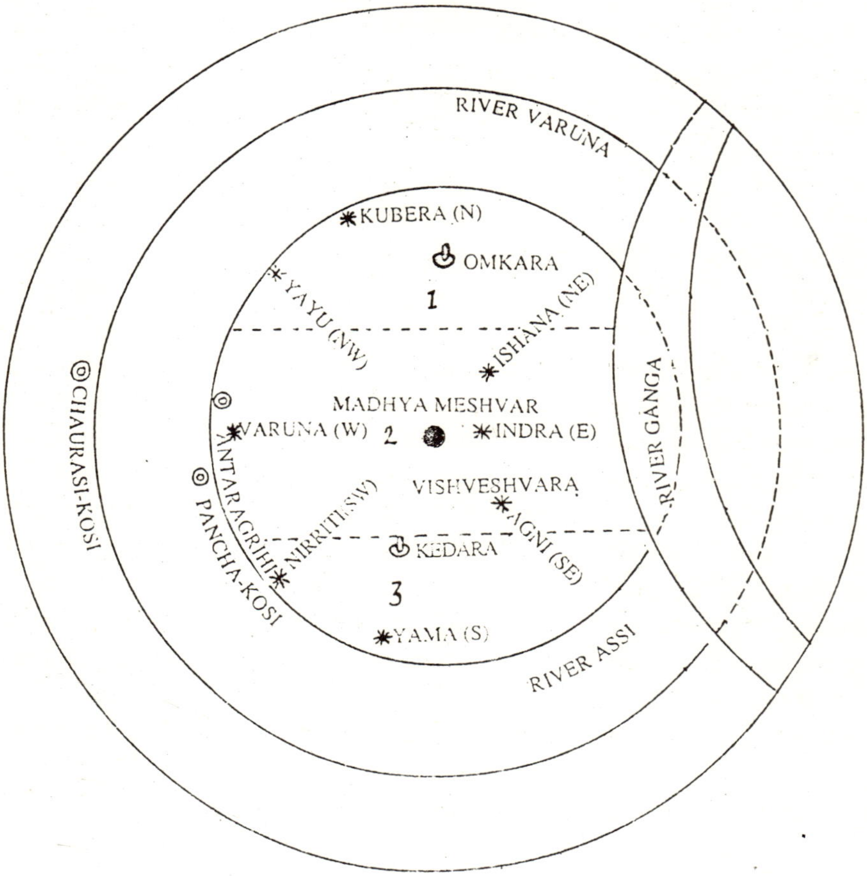

Fig. 7. The Earthly Kashi-*ksetra*

● Lord of the Centre ---- Sector 1, 2, 3 * Directional Guardian
Sector Guardian ◎ Circumambulation

sacred-giving. By dismembering his body and scattering around the necessary number of portions for the completion of the work of creation, *Purusa* established religious rites. From his limbs came the Cosmic Power, the Moon, the Sun, the Fire, the Earth, the Sky, the Air, the points of the compass and everything. Thus the whole world becomes sacred.

The *Puranas* refer to the sacrifice of Dakshiyani or Sati, the daughter of Daksha and the consort of Shiva. It is rooted in the Vedic symbolism. As the scripture describes, her father had organized a big sacrifice (fire ritual) to which all the gods and sages, except Shiva, were invited. She became very angry and gave up her life in protest. The furious Shiva carrying her corpse, went on destroying the life on the Earth. God Vishnu saved the world by dismembering the corpse of Dakshiyani. The various parts of her body fell on earth, each marking the holy place of the Goddess. There are 108 such places. This story of the sacrifice of the Great Mother is a replication of the sacrifice of *Purusa*. Yet another cosmic play which has marked sacred spaces.

The *Skanda Purana* refers to an episode: gods and demons churned the Ocean of Milk. The churning was effected with the Mandara mountain serving as the churn-staff, supported on the back of Vishnu in his tortoise incarnation, while Basuki, the Snake God, served the purpose of rope. The first product of the churning was poison; but as it went on other things emanated: Chandra, the Moon; Kamadhenu, the wish-fulfilling cow; Kalpa, the wish-fulfilling tree with lotus; Kaustubh, the gem; Uchchaishrava, the horse; Airawat, the elephant; and intoxicants like Somarasa; Mahalakshmi, the Goddess of wealth; Pushkar, the airship; Veena, the musical instrument; Rambha, the nymph; Vishvakarma, the architect; and lastly Dhanwantari holding in both his hands the jar of nectar full to the brim. At this Shukracharya, the guru of demons, asked his disciples to seize the jar (*kumbha*) of nectar. That led to a furious battle between gods and demons which lasted for twelve days. In the course of the seize, a few drops of nectar fell from the *kumbha* at twelve places—four on the Earth (Haridwar, Prayaga, Ujjain and Nasik) and eight in the Heaven. The Sun, the Moon and the planet Jupiter were on the vanguard and had protected the jar. The festival of *kumbha* is, therefore, celebrated only on the conjunction of these planets in the sky. As the Gods took twelve days to vanquish the demons and a day of the Gods is equal to a terrestrial year, the *kumbha* recurs at these places every twelfth year in a cyclic order. Six years before and after each *kumbha* comes *ardha* (half) *kumbha*. The place and time of occurrence and the position of planets determining *kumbha* (Table 6) show that the full or half-*kumbha* occurs mainly on the conjunction of the Jupiter with other planets. The half-*kumbha* takes place only at Haridwar and Prayaga. Thus three years after Haridwar another *kumbha* is celebrated at Prayaga. On the sixth year, from the date of *kumbha* at Haridwar or three years after the *kumbha* at Prayag, the festival of *kumbha* is celebrated at Nasik. In the same year, there is a half-*kumbha* at Haridwar and also the *kumbha* at Ujjain. On the ninth year, from the date of Haridwar *kumbha*, or in the sixth year of the last *kumbha* occurs the half-*kumbha* at Prayaga and finally on the twelfth year occurs the full *kumbha* at Haridwar. And this sequence goes on.

TABLE 6: SHOWING THE OCCURRENCE OF *KUMBHA*

Cycle Year	*Place of Occurrence*	*Month of Occurrence*	*Position of Planets*	*Name of Festival*
0	Haridwar	Chaitra (March-April)	Brihaspati (Jupiter) × Kumbha (Aquarius) × Surya (Sun) × Mesha (Aries)	*Kumbha*
3	Prayaga	Magha (Dec.-Jan.)	Brihaspati × Mesha × Surya × Makar (Capricorn)	*Kumbha*
6	(a) Nasik	Chaturmasa (July-Sept.)	Brihaspati × Singha (Leo)	*Kumbha*
	(b) Haridwar	Chaitra (March-April)	Brihaspati × Singha	Ardha *Kumbha*
	(c) Ujjain	Vaisakha (May-June)	Brihaspati × Singha	*Kumbha*
9	Prayaga	Magha (Dec.-Jan.)	Brihaspati × Vrishchik (Scorpion)	Ardha *Kumbha*
12	Haridwar	Chaitra (March-April)	Brihaspati × Kumbha × Surya × Mesha	*Kumbha*

TRANSFORMING PRINCIPLE

From these excellent examples of the cosmic play, the otherwise incomprehensible conception of space as Brahman is realized. Echoes of the cosmic play transform the temporal reality.

The scriptural description of Kashi-*ksetra* may or may not correspond with the empirical reality. Geographically, the shrine of Madhyameshvara does not seem to be the centre of the metropolis Kashi today. But cosmologically it is true that this shrine is the centre not only of Kashi-*ksetra* but for any place in the Universe. Similarly, the holy paths of clockwise circumambulation may not form a perfect circle or triangle or quadrangle, but the pilgrim's movement amplifies all the possible forms of cosmic geometries that give a complete picture of the Universe. Because of the principle of 'self-similarity' a pilgrim visiting Kashi-*ksetra* gets the feeling that he has moved into the boundless cosmic space in all its directions, all its constellations, planets and stars and Gods through the six seasons, driven in the solar car. Residing in Kashi for nine months is like living in the mother's womb. Taking refuge or ending one's life in Kashi means securing salvation and immortality, merging into Brahman—the ultimate goal of pilgrimage.

All places of pilgrimage are the sacred-effective spaces. Entry into a sacred space is an extraordinary event in a man's life. It transforms him completely and brings him closer to the true Self, the Supreme, Soundless, Sacred Brahman. For instance, a pilgrim to the Aiyappa shrine at the Sabari Malai hills in Kerala goes through a remarkable transformation. The mysteries of this pilgrimage are unspeakable but expressible through the pilgrim's ritual act. The pilgrim dies temporally as a secular man and attains the godhood for the time of pilgrimage. He 'becomes' God Aiyappa; his secular personality is switched off. He is addressed as Aiyappa and not by his personal name. Having observed a 30-day vow, the aspirant pilgrim is required to perform a fire-walking ritual to prove that he has followed the rules of conduct fully. Having proven worthy of pilgrimage he breaks a coconut at the doorstep of his house, just before starting the sacred journey. On the way he bathes in River Pumpa and climbs eighteen steps from the feet of the Sabari Malai hills to the shrine. On his assent he breaks a coconut on the relevant step corresponding with the number of his sacred journey to the Aiyappa shrine. All preparatory rituals such as fire-walking, bathing in the river and breaking the coconut symbolize the death of the 'secular man'. Now the pilgrim becomes an 'Aiyappa' and sees the divine bird Garuda and also the self-effulgent light *makaravilaku* across the Sabari Malai hills. This, of course, only a true Aiyappa pilgrim can see and no one else. On the completion of pilgrimage, the pilgrim returns to this-worldly realities and becomes a 'secular man', as before. This is done again in a ritual-way. On his return journey he breaks another coconut on the relevant step in the descending order, bathes in River Pumpa once again and, back home, breaks the last coconut. Thereafter he no longer remains Aiyappa and no one calls him Aiyappa. The ritual of breaking coconut and bathing in the river now symbolizes his return to the normal human state; his re-descent to the temporal world. He regains his secular identity, his name. This extraordinary pilgrimage, involving ritual death and rebirth of the secular man and his transformation as God, is indescribable. The experience of the supreme 'sacred energy' transforming the person is personal.

This is true of the perception of all sacred spaces—transformation of pure energy into form, the form depicting the layered structure of the Universe.

BEYOND THE WORLD OF INNER AND OUTER

There are two models of organization of tradition: one 'inclusive' and the other 'exclusive'. Hinduism represents the inclusive model while Christianity and Islam the exclusive one. The question of 'inner' and 'outer' is vital for the exclusive model. The existence of Christianity, or of Islam, has a meaning only when there are people 'inside' and people 'outside' their fold. The 'inside-outside' makes no sense for an 'inclusive' model. The truth of the unity of all experience and the harmony of all existence was visualized by the ancient cultures.

The Apa Tani's eschatological belief for instance, is quite close to this conception: *Yalo* (soul), of all those who die a natural death goes to Neli, the place of the dead, which looks like an Apa Tani village with long rows of houses. As an Apa Tani lived on this earth, so will he live in Neli—a rich man will find the cattle he has sacrificed during his lifetime, but those animals which have passed to his heirs are for ever lost to him. Every woman returns to her first husband, but those who died unmarried may marry there and beget children. The life in Neli is similar to the life on the earth—people cultivate and work and ultimately they die once more and go to another 'land of the dead'.

The Khasis also believe in continued existence of man's life in a blissful condition. Nothing is so pleasant and entertaining to a Khasi as betel-nut eating in his earthly career. It is believed that after this life when he goes back to the house of God, he would be eating betel-nuts in the company of his near-and-dear ones who have all assembled there.

Nowhere is the unity of 'inner' and 'outer' space expressed so excellently as one finds in this direct intuitive expression and insight. This does not, however, mean that traditional cultures consider all spaces equal in value. The ancient people do differentiate between spaces on the basis of their transforming ability—purity and protection. At the same time they all strive for 'experiencing' the all-embracing unity of space. The ritual spaces and objects are formed or identified separately as places created by gods, demons, or men. The sanctum sanctorum is the most sacred spot; outside are the spaces of a lesser value. When the Muslim iconoclasts of medieval India demolished the shrines and images of gods in the sacred city of Kashi, they thought that they had done away with Hinduism (because all the sacred places and all the images of gods have been polluted and destroyed). But, then, the pandits proclaimed, *kankar kankar me shankar,* 'every pebble of Kashi is God Shankar'. In other words, the distinction of spaces—sacred and secular—is essentially false. Such is also the belief of the Khasis, who choose a site of worship and sanctify it (to what they call *Tang*). However, no such process can be effected without God's permission; which is sought through cock-divination.

In principle and practice, traditional cultures are beyond the world of 'inner' and 'outer'. In their perception, 'fullness' is the essence—the nature of the 'inner' is not different from the nature of the 'outer'. But modern cultures with a strong 'inner' do make a substantive difference between the 'inner' and the 'outer', wanting the 'outer' to transform itself completely to the nature of the 'inner'. The implicit assumption, then, is that the 'inner' is empty and that it needs to be filled in constantly with the 'outer'. Indeed, no culture with strong 'inner'—with a sense of possessing unique elements—can claim eternity.

Chapter 5

The Apperception of Time

MEDITATION UPON TIME

Man's first question was: What is death? That which is unknowable. What is unknowable? That which is unspeakable.

Death, being the first man's first question, is the seed of all knowledge. In the Maithil linguistic tradition, all categories of primal thoughts are expressed by the imagery of death. The terms for the unmanifest, formless, nothingness, darkness, silence, cause, truth and sacred signify death. On the other hand, the words for the manifest, form, thing, light, sound, effect, untruth and non-sacred denote all that *exists*. These two categorical sets are not irreconcilable conflicting binary opposites. They are organically related, ultimately referring to the same phenomenon. Man's second question led him to think that by which events 'take' place — that is, all that *changes*. Human thoughts now get reversed from the visible to the invisible, from the concrete to the abstract, from the knowable to the unknowable and so on. From these two operant ideas emerged the notion of Time (*kala*) and the quest for permanence (*nitya*).

The visible order of the endless repetition of the events of birth and death, light and darkness and sound and silence tacitly affirms the permanence of Time (*nityakala*). The continual act of creation and dissolution, on the other hand, is a clear proof of its impermanence (*anityakala*). The implications, then, are that if there was no change, there would have been no Time and if there was no Time, there would have been no existence. This dialectic of the permanence and impermanence has found its way through all religions, all philosophies and all sciences of the world.

In the Western world, the cycle of the seasons, with its alternating conflict of the hot and the cold, the wet and the dry, seems to have immensely influenced the Greek thinkers. Anaximander (560 BC), who is credited with the discovery of the twelve signs of the zodiac that cause the division of seasons, saw Nature as a continual strife of opposite powers. He associated time with the idea of 'justice' or balance. Permenides, who was the first philosopher to formulate logical proofs rather than dogmatic aphorism and had influenced Plato considerably, asserted that change involves contradiction and so time is irrational, or contrary to reason. The Greek notion of primary opposites came as a turning point in man's perception of the Universe. Nature's destructive force was taken as a challenge to mankind and a new world-view emerged as a consequence. Anaximander became the author of the first scientific cosmogony and first theory of organic evolution.

The biological cycle of human life — birth, old age and death — influenced the Buddha who lived in India about the same time as Anaximander. Like the Greeks, he also realized the tyranny of the ever-changing world and gave a scientific theory of 'dependent origination' (*pratityasamutpada*) that considered man as an aggregate of material factors. But unlike the Greeks, he found the possibility of spiritual progress within the cyclical changes. His 'middle path', the 'path of perfection' (*prajnaparamita*), resolved the problem of conflicting opposites.

Indian tradition has perceived the Universe as a continuum of dynamics between Heaven and Earth. Life and Death are not in opposition; they are the rhythms of biological Time. Biological Time is the rhythm of Cosmic Time and Cosmic Time is the rhythm of the infinite rhythms of transcendental Time. Change is cyclical. But within the cyclical order there is a linear progress and then the layers of progress and decay. Change, at any rate, is not incompatible with progress and existence. Man's relationship with Nature is organic. Nature is just and orderly. There is no cause for man to wage a war against it. Creation (*sristi*), existence (*sthiti*) and dissolution (*pralaya*) are the inexorable Law of Natural Time, each having a divine attribute: truth (*satya*), consciousness (*citta*) and bliss (*ananda*), respectively. The God of destruction, called *Mahakala* — the Great Time — is also auspicious (*Shiva*). Time is fundamental. It creates all forms and destroys them all, but itself remains formless. It transcends everything, but nothing transcends it. It is both linear and cyclical, measurable and immeasurable, with and without quality. What constitutes man and the cosmos is the rhythm of Time.

UPON TIME ALL THE WORLDS REPOSE

The Vedic sages gave a more powerful affirmation of the supremacy of Time. Time stands at the beginning of everything. Time created everything:

> From Time came into being the Waters,
> from Time the Holy Word, Energy and the regions.

By Time (each day) the Sun rises,
in Time he goes to rest again.

By Time blows the cleansing Wind,
through Time the vast Earth has her beings.
The great Heaven has his post in Time.

Their son Time long ago engendered
the things that were and that shall be.
From Time came Scripture into being
and formulas for Sacrifice.

By Time was Sacrifice inaugurated,
inexhaustible oblation to the Gods.
In Time live the spirits and the nymphs.
Upon Time all the worlds repose.

— *Atharvaveda* XIX, 54

The famous invocation of the *Isa Upanisada* says that if from the full one draws away even the full, the full remains. The Vedas interpret this principle as the inexhaustible reality of Time. The vessel set upon Time is so full that however much is drawn from it, Time will never empty it.

Above Time is set a brimful vessel.
Simultaneously we see Time here, there, everywhere.
Set face to face with all existences,
Time is throned, men say, in the loftiest realm.

—*Atharvaveda* XIX, 53

THE WORLD BEYOND TIME

The *upanisadic* sages spoke of two aspects of reality, one temporal and the other non-temporal. The former is cosmological; it is related to the Sun and to the year. The latter is that which remains when everything else dissolves, the timeless Brahman without quality, pure transcendence. Hence the no-time (*akala*) of the *sunya* Brahman, the one in which all that is dead, enters.

Some sages say that inherent nature, others
that Time is this world's cause. Both are mistaken.
It is the grandeur of God within this world
by which this wheel of Brahman is made to turn.

By whom the Universe is ever encompassed, the Knower,
the Author of Time, possessor of all qualities, omniscient.
Ruled by him, the world of creation unfolds—
that which is regarded as earth, water, fire, air and space.

When he has performed this work of creation he ceases,
then enter into union with Being by means of his Being,
by one, two, three or eight categories, by Time
or the subtle qualities that appertain to the *atman*.

—*Svetasvatara Upanisada* VI, 1-3

As many divisions of Time as there are, in all of these moves yonder Sun. From the one who reveres Time as Brahman Time recedes far away. For thus has it been said:

From Time all beings emerge.
From Time they advance and grow.
In Time, too, they come to rest.
Time is embodied and also bodiless.

There are, we aver, two forms of Brahman: Time and the timeless. That which is prior to the Sun is the timeless; it has no parts. That which begins with the Sun, however, is Time and this has parts.

—*Maitri Upanisada* VI, 14-15

COSMOLOGY OF TIME

All timeless people, the cultures believing in eternity, look at the sky as the abode of God(s), the real home of all beings. So the *upanisadic* sages spoke of the 'inverted tree' with roots upward and branches downward. Man as a citizen of the sky and the earth must make no difference.

Whatever is here, that is there,
What is there, that again is here.
He who sees any difference here
goes from death to death.

—*Katha Upanisada* II. 1.10

Man's image of the sky is the same as of himself and of all that is here. The Sun, the Moon, the stars and the planets are the divine manifestations (*vibhuti*), each having a name, a form and an attribute of gods, demons, men and animals (see Table 7). The *rishis*, the ancestors of men, have assumed the form of stars. The Sun and the Moon have kinship with human beings.

Man's rhythm of life is tuned with the sky. His daily routine is organized by the cycle of the Sun; his sustenance by the cycle of the seasons; his joys (festivals) by the cycle of the Moon and so on. Like humans, the citizens of the sky are also governed by the fourfold caste (*varna*) order. In their interpersonal relationship they are also friends, enemies and neutrals. They thrive on man's offerings and oblations.

The sky is the 'book of God', the manual for man. The cosmic cycles are identical with the biological cycles. Life in the sky has patterned the life on the earth. All types of artistic manifestations have a divine origin. These have been revealed, or otherwise brought down from the sky to the earth. All the suns, the moons, the stars, the seasons, the directions, the divisions of time and the countless gods and goddesses, demons, ancestors and primeval sages are enshrined in the holy places all over the earth. The correspondence between the sky and the earth is not in appearance but in operation. They form the cosmic rhythms of time. The Chinese *Tianshi* (Heavenly Time) and the Indian *Mahakala* (Great Time) refer to the same cosmology of time.

TIME BORN WITH SACRIFICE

The smallest fraction of time is called *nimisa*, a Sanskrit word that derives its mythic origin from Nimi, the son of Iksvaku, the grandson of Manu, in the seventh generation of Brahma, the primeval progenitor. In the Maithil tradition, the popular form of myth runs as follows: The king Nimi began the performance of a sacrifice (*yajna*) and appointed Vasistha as priest. Since Vasistha was previously elected as a priest by Indra, the king of Gods, he wanted Nimi to wait till then. But impelled by his desire, Nimi commenced the sacrifice with other priests during the absence of his preceptor, Vasistha. On his return, after having performed that sacrifice of Indra, the preceptor found the transgression on the part of his disciple and so he cursed Nimi, 'May the body of Nimi, who boasts of wisdom, fall'. The body of Nimi fell forthwith. The best of the sages (*munis*) and the gods present at the sacrifice wanted to resuscitate the body of Nimi. But the king who was dead ejaculated saying, 'Let my soul not any more join the body which is the source of perpetual trouble'. On hearing this, the god said, 'Let king Nimi dwell in the eyes of corporeal beings, found only in the winking of eyes, without physical body and existing in the essence of the Self'. The great sages, being apprehensive of anarchy amongst mankind in the absence of a king, then churned the

TABLE 7: THE ATTRIBUTES OF PLANETS

Attributes	*Sun*	*Moon*	*Mars*	*Mercury*	*Jupiter*	*Venus*	*Saturn*
Colour	copper	white	red	green	yellow	mixed (gold and silver)	black
Nature	*sattva*	*sattva*	*tamas*	*rajas*	*sattva*	*rajas*	*tamas*
Sex	male	female	male	eunuch (Female)	male	female	eunuch
Caste	Kshatriya	Vaishya	Kshatriya	Shudra	Brahmana	Candala	Candala
Element	fire	water	fire	earth	ether	water	air
Deity	Agni	Varuna	Subramanya	Vishnu	Indra	Indrani	Brahma
Garment	thick	new	half-burnt	wet	shabby	strong	rag
Metal	copper	gems	gold	brass	silver	pearls	iron (lead)
Part	bones	blood	marrow	skin	flesh and brain	semen	muscles
Grain	wheat	paddy	lentil	green gram	bengal gram	beans	sesamum
Season	summer	winter	summer	autumn	snow	spring	all seasons
Taste	pungent	salt	acerbic	mixed	sweet and cool	sour	bitter and astringent
Residence	place of worship	springs	fire	playground	store-house	bed-chamber	dustbin
Tempera-ment	bilious	phleg-matic	bilious	mixed	phelgmatic	windy and phlegmatic	windy

dead body of Nimi and as a result a son came into being. The said son was called Videha (without body) for his being born from the lifeless body of King Nimi. He had another name of Mithi, as he was born as a result of churning (*manthan*) and the place (now a region) built by this king Mithil is known as Mithila.

The *Rigveda* refers to sacrifice of *Purusa*. From his limbs came all things both animate and inanimate. From his spirit came the Moon, from his eyes the Sun, from his mouth fire, from his feet the earth and from the ears the points of the compass. The poet sages do not mention the term 'time' nor do they elaborate on the nature of time; yet they are not only living in time, but also 'living time'. The origin of Sun and Moon and directions from sacrifice certainly speak of their consciousness of time.

Time was born with the sacrifice and from that the first regnant of Mithila came into being. The smallest fraction of time is called *nimisa*, a Sanskrit word that derives its mythic origin from Nimi. The Vedic Prajapati, the Lord of creatures, is also identified with time. Manu's relationship with ritual is primordial, organic and fundamental. The cosmos is maintained by ritual and ritual, in turn, by a perfect co-ordination between man and time. Man offers sacrifice (ritual) for the preservation of his own life as also of the others. Entering into the sacrifice, the illuminant womb, man and time reach a state of purity (*suddha*) and harmony (*subha*), a phenomenon essential for the well-being of all. Ritual, then, is the proper context of man-time integration. Precisely, it is in this context that man's perception of time can be nearer to what is true. For a man in tradition, properly speaking, there is no time other than ritual time.

FORM OF TIME

According to *Jyotisa* (astrology), time has a form, a heavenly body and a quality. The limbs of the year are named: Prajapati is the head of the year; Visuvata is the body of the year; Viraj is the eye of the year; Phalguni full moon is the mouth of the year; and so on. The twelve signs of the zodiac, respectively, represent the head, face, breasts, heart, belly, navel, abdomen, genital organ, teeth, eyes, knees, anklets and feet of *Kalapurusa*, the Cosmic Time-Person (Fig.8). *Naksatrapurusa* is the lord of the planetary directions. Each sign has a name and a form. The Sun, the Moon, the stars are the Gods; the Great Bear is the constellation of Seven Sages. Then there are the Dragon's Head (Rahu) and the Dragon's Tail (Ketu).

The cycle of the Moon determines the ritual time. The year is made up of twelve moons. There are also twelve suns and twelve zodiac signs that

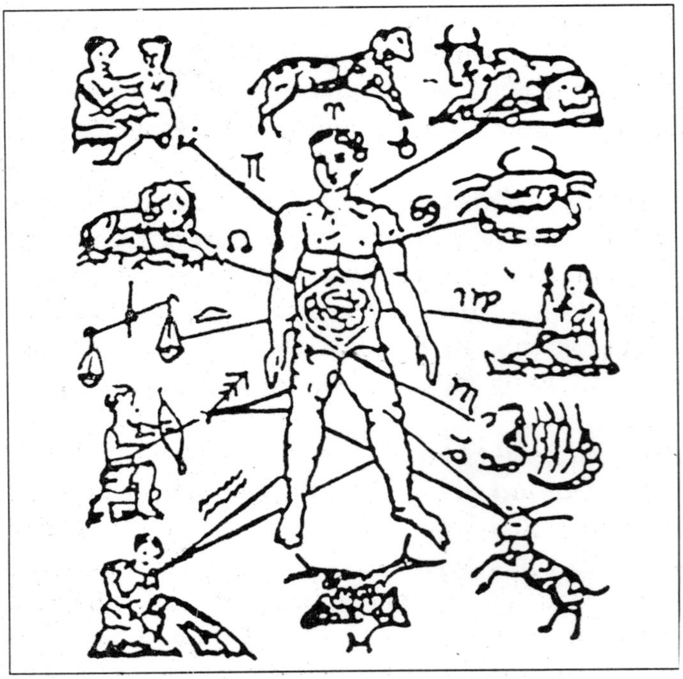

Fig. 8. The twelve signs of the zodiac that form the body of *Kalapurusa*, cause the division of seasons and affect man's future, his rhythms of life, are: Mesa, Vrsa, Mithuna, Karka, Simha, Kanya, Tula, Vrschika, Dhanu, Makara, Kumbha, Mina

make up the body of the Time-Person. Time has a form, a heavenly body and a quality. The limbs of the year are named. The planets have distinctive spheres and uneven quality: some are benefic and some malefic. Their disposition and relation values are calculated to construct a horoscope (Greek: *hora,* time, *skopos,* observer), to guide human activities. The almanac (*pancanga*, five limbs) serves a twofold purpose; it schedules the religious ceremonies and records the cosmic events in due consideration of lunar-solar-stellar situations. The five limbs of time are: *tithi*, day of the moon: *vara*, a day of the sun: *naksatra*, the stellar position; *yoga*, favourable or unfavourable time determined by the relation of the Sun and Moon and *karna*, a unit (half) of the lunar day. The other contents of the almanac, in respect of each lunar day and the corresponding solar day, are the position of the Moon and the Sun in the zodiac, total duration of the day, the sunrise, the sunset and the first rising sign of the zodiac. The lunar month of thirty days, fortnight, the era (*Vikrama Samvata*, beginning in 58 BC; *Saka*, beginning in AD 592); season, solstice, quadrant, the mid-point of the year, cosmic ages, aeon, etc. are scrupulously recorded. The qualitative descriptions of time such as the divinity of the year, the horoscope of the year, the auspicious time for domestic rituals, agricultural operations, house-building, etc., are given. All the prescribed rituals, festivals and fasts, the astronomical tables, the appropriate sacred words for ritualistic performances and such other useful information are provided in the almanac.

Biological time of a man begins from birth. In *Jyotisa,* birth is determined in three ways: (1) the moment of appearance of the head, (2) the moment of appearance of the tip of the nose, (3) and the moment of the parturition of the child. The position of the planets must be noted according to the second. In practice, however, the third alone constitutes birth.

The *Jyotisa* texts proclaim that he who makes the study of almanac becomes free from all sins; knowledge of *tithi* brings prosperity; knowledge of *vara* prolongs life; knowledge of *naksatra* causes the destruction of the sins; knowledge of *yoga* gives immunity from disease; and knowledge of *karna* leads to success in all endeavours.

Among the Maithils, the more common expressions for human lifespan are 'a spidery thread', 'a tree', 'a river' and 'a lamp', imagining progression with occasional sidetracks. Time is like a spider's web (angular); like a tree with branches spread out; like a river with tributaries progressing relatively in relation to the surface of the earth; or like a lamp flickering; but *not* an arrow-like movement. This vision of time is incompatible with the Newtonian notion: 'Absolute, true and mathematical time, of itself and from its own nature, flows equably without relation to anything external'. In Indian perception, time has a form. The *Puranas* have mentioned *Kalatirtha*, time in the form of sacred. Certain days and months are considered sacred. Their merits are also self-formed. There are several other forms of time.

These forms are measurable. Propitious moment (*muhurta*) for an event is subject to mathematical measurement. The Sun and the Moon are the universal clock. There are ways of measuring the duration of ritual time for which no almanac is required. Ritual itself is a clock. By uttering the desired number of *mantra*, by reading a scripture and by using instrument, the ritual time is measured. By increasing the number of performers, the ritual time can be accelerated; by successive performances over a long period of time, it can be accumulated. Since time is cumulative, merits in lifetime accumulate — *punya sancaya* is the Maithili expression.

Rituals are scheduled and observed daily; on different days of the fortnight; in different months of the year; different seasons of the year; under the auspices of different asterism; and on the occasions of the Sun's passing over a new zodiac sign. The junctures of the day (*sandhya*) are important for the recitation of the *gayatri mantra*. The duration of ritual time may vary from a few minutes (as seeing the image of God) to several years (as in the case of the Vedic *yajna*). The life-cycle rituals are scheduled on the occurrence of birth and death and in between at various stages in life. Calendrical rituals are repeated every year. Certain rituals are in a twelve-year cycle and even once in many years. For instance, the festival of *Kumbha* is performed every twelfth year in cyclical order. The wooden body of the image of Lord Jagannath of Puri is changed every twelfth year. The bathing ritual of *Ardhodaya* occurs when in the month of *Pausa* (December/January) or Magh (January/February) a new Moon falls on Sunday and the rising constellation is *Sravana* during daytime and the *yoga* is *Vyatipata*. This takes place at regular intervals. The eclipse of the Sun and the Moon recurs periodically.

There are in ritual times discontinuous series. All *tithis* are not ritually important. Some are significant in both the bright and the dark halves, such as the *Ekadasi*. But all *Ekadasis* are again not of equal merit. Two most important of them are the time when the Vishnu wakes up and when he goes to sleep for four months. All life-cycle rituals cannot be performed round the year. Celebration of marriage must be avoided in the inauspicious months and on Saturday, Sunday and Tuesday. The restricted period of marriage ceremony called *aticara* may sometimes extend over a year.

Such intervals of the varying duration, determined by astral consideration, show that time cannot be fitted into a simple linear cause-effect relation. By stretching the linear timescale, a pattern of cyclical events emerges. The cosmic cycle flows into the linear evolution of life and the linear lifespan returns, through death, to the cosmic cycle and thus it goes on endlessly. Geologic time is also perceived as cyclical at the macro-level but appearing linear at the micro-level of interaction.

EXPERIENCING TIME

Ritual is an event of experiencing time in its fullness: a consideration which has developed the complex system of interlocking the abstract (ordinal duration) and the concrete (living nature), the celestial (astral) and the terrestrial (social) order. For example—

ORDER AND DURATION

Ritual fast associated with Monday is observed on all Mondays in the month of *Sravana* (July/August) from *Sankranti* (Sun's passing over a new zodiac sign) to *Sankranti*; and during the remaining part of the year only when Monday falls on a new Moon day.

DURATION, EVENT AND NUMBER

No three auspicious ceremonies (such as marriage, sacred thread, etc.) can be performed within a period of six months.

NUMBER, RITUAL-ORDER AND TIME-ORDER

The ancillary rites of sacrifice, marriage and tonsure must begin twenty-one days, ten days and three days, respectively, ahead of the appointed day of the main ritual.

GENDER, NUMBER AND DURATION

Tonsure, sacred thread, or marriage ritual of two uterine brothers or sisters, must not be performed within a year.

GENDER AND BIOLOGICAL TIME

Marriage to be celebrated in the fifth, sixth or seventh year in the case of the female; and in the case of the male on attaining puberty.

BIOLOGICAL TIME AND ASTRAL POSITION

The *pumsavanam* ritual is observed when as woman is in the third, sixth or eighth month of pregnancy under the asterism *Pusya* or *Sravana*. Biological time begins from the moment of birth.

BIOLOGICAL ORDER (OF BIRTH) AND ASTRAL ORDER (of year)

Marriage of the eldest son or daughter must not be performed in the month of Jyestha (May/June).

SOCIAL ORDER (CASTE) AND ASTRAL ORDER (day)

Among malefic days of tonsure, Sunday is favourable for Brahmana; Tuesday for Kshatriya; and Saturday for Vaishya and other castes.

KINSHIP ORDER, DURATION, GENERATION TIME AND GREAT TIME (death)

On an auspicious occasion, if there is a death in the kin's group, within four generations, then the *Nandisradha* ritual must not be observed until the entire course of the death rites is complete.

MULTIPLE TIME SYSTEMS

There is no universal time covering all ritual events occurring everywhere through every individual. Ritual time is not only discontinuous but also dependent on multiple time orders. Traditions of rituals are varied. Besides, there are different systems of time-reckoning even within a single tradition.

The working principle of the *Vedanga Jyotisa* differs from the *Siddhanta Jyotisa*. The Brahmana year begins from spring; the Kshatriya year from summer and the Vaisya year from autumn. Scriptures and oral traditions are many and hence the forms and ways of ritual are varied. Ritual has a spiritual value for all Hindus, but not all rituals have a Hindu-wide performance.

Rituals are observed at a relative gap in due consideration of caste, age, sex and place. A Brahmana performs the naming ritual of the child on the twelfth day of the birth, a Kshatriya on the sixteenth day; a Vaishya on the twentieth day; and a Shudra on the twenty-second day. The child's tonsure is performed in the third, fifth or seventh year from the date of its birth. For a male child, the 'feeding-on-rice' ritual is observed in the sixth month; for a female the fifth month. When a girl is about to reach puberty, the rules about certain planetary combinations bestowing adverse influence on marriage are not applicable in the tract lying between the Ganga and the Gomati — the two great rivers.

In view of the multiplicity of temporal time-systems, even if the astral time is the same, the ritual time for two observers may be different. Ritual time is derived from event and the event is dependent on the temporal order (caste, age, sex, place, etc.). The order of ritual time therefore, changes by change in the cultural order. Due to this special (cultural) relativity, which is similar to Einstein's theory of relativity, ritual time cannot be brought into a single objective time sequence. This evident temporality of ritual time goes well with Shankaracharya's celebrated claim and philosophical insight that time (*kala*) is a temporal phenomenon (*vyavaharika*) and not a basic element (*tattva*).

SPACE-TIME

Like time, space is of uneven quality. All places are not suitable for sacred performances; some are more sacred-effective than others. The effectiveness of a space depends on its association with Gods, sages, ancestors and primeval events. A place is consecrated by the powers of the sacred-word (*mantra*). Even within the sacred-spaces, there are 'purity space' and 'protection space', each endowed with efficient power but functionally different from one another. Ritual event takes (ritual) place. Ritual time and ritual space are inextricably bound together.

Direction and time are also interrelated. The *Jyotisa* prescribes the rules relating to travel. It gives not only the proper day and time but also the proper direction in relation to time for starting on a journey. The points of the horizon are governed by what is known as *yogini* during the bright and dark halves of the lunar month. The location of *yogini* at the time of starting on a journey is an important matter. *Yogini* located behind or on the right hand direction of the traveller, is conducive to success; the *yogini* in front or on the left side of the person proves disastrous. There is also a consideration of *rasi*, the sign of the zodiac and their direction. One should choose Aries, to go eastward; Cancer, to go southward; Libra, to go westward; and Capricorn, to go northward. There are planetary directions. The day is divided into eight parts of an hour-and-half each. Each part is called *yamam*. To start on a journey at a moment when *Kala*, the Lord of Death, governs the direction in which the person has to travel, gives victory over enemies. The days of the week are also considered for travel. It is inauspicious to go south-east on Tuesday, south-west on Wednesday and north-west on Saturday.

Consideration of time is an important matter for all such events as constructing a house or a temple, etc. The sacred effectiveness of a ritual act increases manifold on the interpenetration of space and time. For instance, bathing in a sacred river at any time, or bathing in a river at an auspicious time, is endowed with merit. But bathing in the confluence of the three rivers—the Ganga, the Yamuna and the Saraswati—at Prayaga during Kartik (October/November) has inexhaustible merit. Kashi, as a spiritually perceived microcosm, enshrines not only all the sacred places (*tirthas*) on the earth but also all the heavenly bodies: all the suns, moons, the stars and the planets, the seasons and all the divisions of time in their essence. Hence pilgrimage to this place is praiseworthy.

All the bathing rituals and festivals are observed on special occasions in ritual space-time. This agrees with Minkowski's theory that 'Henceforth space by itself and time by itself, are doomed to fade away into mere shadows and only a kind of union of the two will preserve an independent reality'.

ACT-ORDER-TIME

Ritual act (*karma*), order (*krama*) and time (*kala*) are aspects of Great Act (*mahakarma*), Primeval Creation, Great Order (*mahakrama*), Primeval Preservation Great Time (*mahakala*) and Primeval Dissolution. They are inconceivable without one another. It can be understood best by the analogy of body, mind and spirit. Each one of these is subject to the contingent process of the world system. Their essential connection lies in the fact that an act is realized only by the virtue of the order that occurs to create the capacity for time. Thus, in a ritual complex, order is the crucial element from which both act and time assume their form and by which they unite.

Worship (*puja*) is an act of honour-offerings to a deity. The honour-offering is of two kinds: one called *sodasopacara* (the sixteen-offering), another *pancopacara* (the five-offering). Their difference is ordinal. The sixteen-offering begins with the first element invocation (*avahana*) and ends at the sixteenth, completion (*visarjana*). They form a continuum of sixteen orders, each having a set of numerous micro-elements, or properties, of offerings, in accord with the 'ritual language'. In the 'invocation', for instance, the micro-elements are the sacred words (*mantra*) by which the deity is invoked; the articles such as holy water and flowers; the ritual instruments such as spoon, holy grass, bell or conch; the hand gestures (*mudras*) and so on. The ritual manual provides the correct procedure in which the orders are to occur. It refers to such considerations as to whether the flowers should be offered first, or the garland; the sandal paste first, or sesame (*tila*), or unbroken rice (*aksata*); oblation (*arghya*) first, or bathing, or sipping (*acamana*); and so on. All the sixteen offerings occur in a non-hierarchic succession. The micro-elements within each of them are not disposed to a chronological order. While reciting a *mantra*, the observer may hold a *mudra* and create a sound (*dhvani*) by ringing the bell simultaneously. Offerings of flowers, water, unbroken rice, sesame, holy leaves, etc. may sometimes be made separately; sometimes in multiple combinations; but never are they arbitrarily chosen. Each element is valuable. Together they make the worship meaningful, aesthetically pleasing and structurally suitable for man-God union. The sixteen offerings make the total lifespan of the worship, where invocation is the birth and completion is the death; the other fourteen offerings in between are the points of growth. The ordinal aspect of the worship-time is determined by such considerations of micro-elements as to how many times the flowers are to be offered or the sacred words to be recited or the lamps to be waved and so on. Metaphorically speaking, the texture of a worship-time is woven by the warps of fixed length and numerous wefts of the micro-elements that fill the ritual space-time.

Thus ritual time is not an independent reality; it is set into motion by a linear continuum of orders, within which change occurs in *kairological* moment and not in a linear chronological order. The fruit (*parinama*) of worship is neither the sum-total nor the geometric progression of the order. The sixteen orders of the worship are the sixteen kinds of present, occurring in a sequence. They all are important for the enactment of worship but the fruit of worship is not dependent on them. The order of circumambulation signifies the cyclic order by which all the preceding linear orders are contained. The sixteenth order (completion) signifies the dissolution of all that was present. In the situation, the fruit of worship occurs only in 'no-time', in *kairological* moment, the rhythm of Great Time, the leap into timelessness (Sanskrit, *ksna*, Chinese, *shih*), the true state of consciousness.

To clarify further: Like the sixteen-offerings, meditation is also a kind of worship; its desired fruit is also the same as that of the former. But the duration and order of time in either case are very different. As the Hindu scripture reveals: by meditating upon the Self for thirteen winks (*nimisa matra*), one gets the same fruit as acquired from the ritual offering of a cow; for a 100-wink, the fruit of making horse-sacrifice (*asvamedha yajna*); a half-hour meditation brings as much merit as from 1,000 horse-sacrifice. An hour of meditation deserves a higher merit of sacrifice (*rajasuya yajna);* a half-day meditation rewards one lakh *rajasuya yajna*; and a day leads to the ultimate goal (*paramadhama*) of human life. The obvious intention here is to say that the fruit of a long-drawn performance is achieved in 'no-time'.

What really matters in ritual time, then, is not the ordinal duration but the spiritual moment (*cinamatra*) associated with the Infinite that presents itself (*suksma pratyaksa*) to effect or affect the event (finite time). This moment is the 'pure experiential time' of a yogi; in it the past, the present and the future are fused into one. It is possible for a yogi to speak of the past event, to predict the future and to create objects or events 'out of time' (*akrama srsti*), precisely because he can see and live that moment (*yogi-pratyaksa*) which remains unmanifest, unknown for the common man.

Thus, the fruit of ritual time occurs on the concatenation and *not* at the completion (ordinal duration) of the orders. The factor that selects the 'efficient moment' out of a great number of possible stages in the orders of human act remains unknown.

TRANSCENDENCE OF TIME

There are beliefs and ritual ways of reversing time Many years ago, as the story goes, one pandit Dhiren Upadhya began performing a sacrifice proper to the consecration of a new tank at his village in Mithila. As the ritual was coming to an end, he detected a mistake in his performance. The Sun was about to set and there was no possibility of his re-doing the ritual within the proper time, that is, before the sunset. Moreover, this lapse would have caused him a deadly sin. Impelled by anxiety, he used his spiritual powers to halt the movement of the Sun forthwith. The full ritual was recommenced while the Sun was still up in the sky. After the performance, the power of the *mantra* was withdrawn and the Sun disappeared. By that time, three-fourth of the night had already passed.

There are other examples found in the Indian tradition. To guard against the dangers of eclipse-time, a pregnant woman is measured by a stick equal of her height; the stick is kept in a dark room where she is made to stay. A pregnant cattle is also protected by drawing a circle, with red ochre, around her belly. This is how the adverse effects of the eclipse-time are neutralized.

The *gayatri mantra* is performed in the morning, midday and evening, on the juncture of time called *sandhya*. It is set into ten orders, marked by various gestures (*mudras*) and sacred words (*mantras*). The ritual order of the performance is fused by the repetition of the kinetic order of right and left (hands, shoulders, nostrils). The sequence of invocation to deities reflects progression rather than a sacred order (hierarchy). It begins with the propitiation of *Rishis* and then to the black Vishnu, to the red Vishnu, to the white Shiva, to *Rishis* again and finally to Gayatri, the principal deity of worship. The order symbolizes the forward movement from darkness to light. The *Rishis* are symbolic representation of Brahma, the progenitor. They are identified with immortality.

THE PRESENCE OF FUTURE TIME

Every year, Goddess Durga visits men on the Earth during *Sardiya Navaratra* (September/October). The vehicle used for her earthly journey foretell the future events affecting man's life (Table 8).

TABLE 8: THE VEHICLES OF THE GODDESS DURGA

	Day	*Vehicle*	*Consequence*
Arrival	Sun., Mon.	elephant	flood
	Sat., Tues.	horse	disaster to the regnant
	Thurs., Fri.	palanquin	death
	Wed.	boat	success
Departure	Sun., Mon.	buffalo	sickness and sorrow
	Sat., Tues.	cock	chaos
	Wed., Fri.	horse	good rain
	Thurs.	man	auspicious

GREAT TIME

All existence is time. But ritual time is different; it is rooted in non-existence. The ultimate goal of all rituals is to transcend 'temporal time' (*anityakala*).

Ritual time must, therefore, reflect the aspect of the Great Time (*mahakala, nityakala*). Here are some examples.

Ritual Creation and Dissolution

In the clay image of a deity, the life-force is infused by a method proper to life-invoking (*prana pratistha*) and on the completion of the worship it is ritually terminated (*visarjana*). Women observe a certain ritual by which they believe to have prolonged the biological time of their husbands, sons and brothers. A sannyasi performs his own funeral rites which signify his death as a worldly individual. By performing a certain ritual, the Indian peasants neutralize the dangerous effects of the eclipse-time. A mystic stops the motion of the Sun by his spiritual powers.

Dissolution of the Temporal Order of Time

Symbolic transcendence of past, present and future is observed in a ritual context. During the dark fortnight of Asvina (October/November), called *pitripaksa*, the ancestors are invoked to be physically present to be treated sumptuously. Death in a 'timeless people' fails to break the human ties of kinship. Deities are invoked to be physically present. The presence of the deity means the presence of the future. The vehicle used by the Goddess Durga for her arrival and departure indicates the future on the Earth. The mystics speak truth by reversing the order of language. Kabir, a medieval saint, thus spoke in the verse called *ulatabansi*, the inverted flute. The *gayatri mantra* is recited at the juncture of time (*sandhya*), signifying transcendence of the division of time into day and night.

Transformation of Man into God

In the 'Virgin Worship' (*kumari puja*), a three - or five - or seven-year-old girl represents the Goddess Durga. While honour-offerings are made to her, she is temporarily transformed, as in *lila*, into Durga and thereafter she regains her status and identity of a human child. A pilgrim to the Aiyappa shrine undergoes a similar process of transformation. He is called Aiyappa for the entire period of pilgrimage. He regains his secular identity, his name, only on the completion of the sacred journey.

Experiencing the Rhythms of Great Time

The Hindu almanac mentions the date of the beginning and the end of the first three cosmic ages (*yuga*), the beginning of the Kali *Yuga*, the birthday of all the incarnations of Vishnu, other divine events of the past, etc. These are observed as ritual time. At the beginning of a ritual, the performer makes a vow of determination (*samkalpa*) and defines the present instant of performance by recounting the primordial time and the space-time. Circumambulation of the Kashi-*ksetra*, which enshrines the presiding deities (*adhidevata*) of all times and seasons,. all sacred spaces and all divinities, helps the performer realize the rhythms of cosmic space-time. Death in Kashi or in Ujjain, the city of *Mahakala*, is auspicious because thereby the deceased person is freed from the cosmic cycle of time and seasons, biological cycle of birth and death and from all orders and functions of worldly-life for ever and ever. He becomes one with the *Mahakala*.

Expressing the Symbol of Great Time

The difference between the temporal time and the Great Time may be summed up. The former is characterized by act, order and time; the latter by no-act (*akarma*), no-order (*akrama*) and no-time (*akala*). *Kala* (Time) and *Mahakala* (Great Time) are intrinsically connected. Goddess Kali or *Mahakali* (the Great Energy of Time), is the consort of *Mahakala*, the Great Time. The awareness of this truth is reflected in the acceptance of lunar time by all the 'timeless people'. It finds its finest expression in Indian art. It shows the visual image of the Moon (the lunar time), the Ganga (the flow of time) adorning the matted hair (the spidery thread of time) and Kalavyala (the serpent of time) hanging round the neck of *Mahakala* (the Great Time), the Creator of creators, the Preserver of preservers, the Destroyer of destroyers, the nameless, the formless, the unknowable one whose mere spiritual vibrations can be felt in Kashi, the Avimuktaksetra — the place never forsaken – by Shiva Viswanatha, the auspicious Lord of the Universe.

THE SEVEN SUTRAS

What follows from the foregoing description of the vision and tradition of time are the seven operant threads (*sutra*), clearly visible.

First

Man, Time and Space are ritually constructed. Ritual is an aspect of the Cosmic Law/Order (*Rta*) that transcends all laws; causes the birth and death of all corporeal beings, all things and events; and holds the cosmos by its own power. Whatever is created in Time dissolves naturally into the Great Time. Ritual time is impermanent because it takes place in temporal time; but all rituals are aimed at permanence. There is an essential connection between Time and Great Time. Ritual Time mediates between Time and Great Time. To a man in tradition there is no time other than Ritual Time.

Second

Ritual Time is determined by the cosmic clock. Ritual itself is a clock. Since Time is born—like other corporeal beings and things—it has a form and quality. Time, as a form and quality, is measurable, discontinuous and cumulative. Man schedules his time by interlocking of the abstract (ordinal duration) and the concrete (living nature), of the celestial (astral) and the terrestrial (social).

Third

Ritual Time is observed at a relative rest in due consideration of caste, age, sex and place. The order of ritual changes by change in the order of the observer. This special relativity of ritual time is caused by the temporality of man, the observer. Ritual becomes a high-order sacred-effective act only when observed in ritual space-time. Time and space are inextricably linked. Space-time is a spidery thread woven into a linear-cyclical order.

Fourth

Act (*Karma*), Order (*Krama*) and Time (*Kala*) are inconceivable without one another. Act is realized by virtue of Order that occurs to create a capacity to Time. Time is not an independent reality. It is set into motion by a linear continuum of Order within which changes occur in *kairological* moment and not in a chronological order.

Fifth

No-Act (*Akarma*), No-Order (*Akrama*) and No-Time (*Akala*) are the aspects of Great Time (*Mahakala*). Man is impelled by his desire to seek immortality, a primordial state of permanence. Man's quest for return to the primordial is reflected in his ritual behaviour—archetypal creation and dissolution of time experience the *kairological* moment as the rhythm of Great Time.

Sixth

Change, being the Law of Time, exists. Its existence is caused in the same way as in the case of all that exists. Death (Great Time) causes change; it transcends Time but nothing transcends it.

SEVENTH

Cosmocentric Man transcends temporal Time in a ritual context that situates him in a perfect harmony with Nature and makes his experience of the transcendence real. Technocentric man ventures to transcend temporal Time in a mundane context that takes him nowhere, situates him in a continual strife (direct confrontation) with Nature and makes his expression of transcendence unreal.

Chapter 6

The Ontology of Mind

WHAT IS MIND? WHO IS IT?

The Vedic seers were overwhelmed by the power of the Word, which means revelation. The *upanisadic* sages enquired: whose is the Word? The revelation cannot be reduced to a single one of its dimensions. This led to a great deal of thinking about the Mind.

ORIGIN

The *Rigveda* (X.129) reveals: 'In the beginning love arose which was the primal germ cell of the Mind'. The *Atharvaveda* (XIX.52) holds: 'Desire was the First seed of Mind'. The *Satapatha Brahmana* (X.5.3.1-5) explains it further: This Universe was neither Being nor Non-being; only Mind was there. This Mind, so to speak, was neither existent nor non-existent. That Mind created the Word, the Word created the life breath.

MATTER AND LIFE

The *Prasna Upanisada* (1.4-5) tells us that 'The Lord of Creature (Prajapati) tells us produced a pair, Matter and Life. Now, Life is the Sun, Matter is the Moon. Matter is all this, the formed and the formless'. The *Kaushitaki Upanisada* (III.2-3) brings forward the details: 'Life is temporal and temporal life is Life. Life is also immortality. For as long as life remains in the body there is temporal life. Life is consciousness and consciousness is Life. When a sick person is about to die, he loses consciousness. People say to him: his Mind has departed, he neither hears nor sees nor speaks words nor thinks, then he is absorbed into life. Then speech together with all names is absorbed, the eye together with all forms, the ear together with all sounds and the Mind together with thoughts go to it. And when he departs from his body, he departs together with all these'.

MIND AND THE SELF

The *Brihadaranyaka Upanisada* (3.9.13) claims that 'He who knows that Person whose abode is space, whose world is the ear, whose light is Mind, who is the source of every soul – he, verily, would be a knower'. The *Prasna Upanisada* (6.4) takes it further: 'He (i.e. the Person) emitted life: from Life came faith, then space, wind, light, water, earth, sense-faculty, mind, food; from food, virility, austerity, sacred sayings, sacrifice, the worlds and in the worlds, name, i.e. the individual'. In the *Chandogya Upanisada* (VIII.3.1) it is said: 'Mind is greater than Word; it grasps both Word and name. Mind is the *atman*, Mind is the Word, Mind is certainly Brahman. Meditate on Mind'. The *Katha Upanisada* (III.13) enjoins: 'The wise man should surrender his words to his mind and thus he should surrender to the Knowing Self'. The *Brihadaranyaka* (III.7.20) discloses: 'He who dwells in the Mind, yet is other than Mind, whom the Mind does not know, whose body is the Mind, who controls the Mind from within—he is the *atman* within you, the Inner Controller, the Immortal'.

MIND AND BODY

The *Taittiriya Upanisada* (3.1.3) proclaims that 'Beings here are born from Mind, when born they live by Mind, on deceasing they enter into Mind'. In *Katha Upanisada*'s (3.3.4) view, 'The body is a chariot, the intellect is the chariot driver, the Mind is the reins and the senses the horses. The self, combined with senses and Mind, is the enjoyer'. For *Brihadarnyaka* (1.5.3), 'Mind is the agent in all conscious experience such as seeing, hearing, imaging, doubting, believing, fearing, meditating and so on'. *Taittiriya* (1.6.1) states explicitly: 'The body consists of Mind. Within the body, there is a lotus-shaped piece of flesh called the heart. The space within the heart is the permanent seat of the Mind'. The *Chandogya* (VI.8.1-2) clarifies the relationship between the Mind and Life: 'Just as a bird, tied to a string, after flying about in different directions and not finding any other resting place, finally finds a perch in the place of its captivity, so also the Mind after flying about in different directions and not finding any other resting place finally finds a support in the breath of life, for the Mind is tied to the breath of life'.

To understand the *upanisadic* science, one has to bear in mind that the Cosmic Order (*rta*) is not to be equated with modern scientific law of Nature. In it, there is no such thing as biological evolution. There are two fundamental principles: Matter and Life, which causes the origin of all. The Matter enters into the composition of all beings. Life possesses an ontological rather than a psychological function. Here the terms are given cosmological symbolism: Matter is the Moon and Life is the Sun. Matter is the formed and the unformed structure of reality. Life is not that which gives form but that which gives existence.

It is hard to separate Mind from Matter. Mind is the formless Matter. Mind created the Word; the Word created the life in which everything is established. The universal life consists of Matter. Life is temporal and it is also immortal. There is also the universal Mind, the Mind of mind, the Mother of mind. Beings are born from Mind, when born they live by Mind and at death they return to Mind. Mind is located in the heart. Mind is the Self (*atman*). Mind is Brahman, the Ultimate Reality.

Reading the sacred texts, it may appear at the first sight that they are a bundle of paradoxes (e.g. in the beginning there was neither Being nor Non-being: only Mind was there, neither existent nor non-existent); and also inconsistencies in sequencing (e.g. Mind created the Word, Word created Life; from Life came faith, then Mind). To this, it can be said that revelation is not evolution. What is presented in these texts is the insight of the oneness of the *real* reality. The unveiling of depths has a value that is independent of human imagination. As has been said, Mind follows faith, faith follows the heart where Mind is seated. The unity of Mind (*manas*) and Wisdom (*buddhi*) follows the Light of the Self.

WHAT IS MAN? WHO IS HE?

The key feature of *upanisadic* thinking concerns the essential oneness of the individual self and the universal Self. The Vedic seers gave a cosmological conception of Man.

ORIGIN

The *Rigveda* (X.9) reveals the origin of the primordial Man: a thousand-headed Man with a thousand eyes, a thousand feet; encompassing the earth from all the sides, he exceeded by ten fingers 'breath'. From him the shining one was born. From that one Man again took birth. Using the Man as their oblation, the Gods performed the sacrifice. From the sacrifice of the Cosmic Man, came all things – both animate and inanimate; animals of every type; liturgical formulas; the four castes of man; and the cosmic powers. From his spirit comes the Moon, from his eyes, the Sun; from his mouth; the fire; from his breath, the wind; from his head, the sky; from his feet, the earth; from his ears, the four directions.

MAN AND MIND

The *Taittiriya Upanisada* (2.1.5) mentions that 'Man is enveloped by five sheaths. He consists of the essence of food, breath, Mind, understanding and bliss'. The *Maitri Upanisada* (VI.34.1-11) specifies further : 'Mind is of two kinds: pure and impure. It becomes impure when it is touched by desire and pure when freed from desire. When a man, having made his mind perfectly stable, free from attachment and confusion, enters upon the mindless state, then he attains the supreme abode. The Mind alone is Man's cause of bondage or release: it leads to bondage when attached to the sense objects and to release when free from them'. For Kabir, the medieval saint poet, 'He who walks between boundaries is Man, he who goes beyond them is saint. But he who transcends the limited and the limitless, his Mind is unfathomable'. Chandidas presents an anthropocentric view: 'Man is Truth above all things. There is nothing above him'. Kabir highlights the power of Mind: The body is a pitch-dark forest and Mind is an elephant gone mad. The Jewel of Wisdom is the goad but few are the saints who can apply it. The Three Worlds were plundered, they all were stripped of their all. But Mind is a faceless thief, whom no one could recognize. The body is the temple, the Mind is the banner fluttering in the wind of sensual desire. The pull of the Mind shakes the temples and it is totally destroyed. The Mind is aware of all and, knowingly, it does wrong. Will you fare any better, if you fall into a well with a lamp in hand? Defeat of the Mind is the real defeat, victory over the Mind is the real victory. Strike the mad elephant Mind, force it inside the body. And if it turns round and runs away, bring it back again with the goad. The Mind is like a bird; rising, it flew to the sky. Then it fell down from there again into the noose of *maya*. Stretching your body as a bow, making the 'five elements' your arrows, shoot down that deer Mind, or else your wisdom is false. A crack has come into my Mind, a very, very deep crack. Just like a broken marble slab, that will never join together. Follow not the guidance of the Mind, forgetting the soul's true nature. As the thread upon the spindle, reverse and wind it back.

MIND AND *MAYA*

Kabir characterizes the state of Mind, pointing out that '*Maya* is an enchantress, who tricks the wisest of the sages. *Maya* is an ogress, she eats up everything. Stronger than a chain (of iron) is *Maya* in this world. How could any poor creatures escape her, when the creator has chained them down? Deluded by *Maya*, the whole world went blind. *Maya* is a tree made of suffering; the branches are the torment of the senses. It gives no coolness, even in dreams, its fruit is insipid and poisonous. *Maya* never died nor died the Mind, but body after body kept dying. Desire and thirst never died. *Maya* is the lamp, Man is the moth, circling around the flame he falls. *Maya* dwells within the Mind'.

The Sacred Science mirrors the mystery of Man and Mind splendidly. Man is an aspect of the whole of reality. His origin from the sacrifice of *Purusa*, the primordial man, makes him a ritual being. He is fivefold: made up of five elements (earth, water, fire, air and sky), five material factors (food, breath, mind, understanding and bliss). Looked at from the Buddhist point of view, there are multiple bodies. Man is both bounded and boundless. Ḥe is made of Mind (*moner manus*). It is the Mind which gives him a personal structure, a higher or a lower state, the inner and the outer environment. The inner Man is ever wakeful, ever active and ever pure. By realizing the truth that the higher Self is hidden in his body, Man becomes immortal. Then, there is nothing above him. But a cunning Mind is the worst enemy of Man. He who succeeds in stilling the Mind becomes the creator himself. The cunning Mind of modern Man is an elephant gone mad. The saint, a true yogi, is compared to an elephant's goad which is able to control the furious elephant of the Mind. He guides common Man to come out of the forest of desire. Such a saint is rare. *Maya* dwells within the Mind; Man is deluded by *maya*. Body is the puppet.

WHAT IS MASK? WHO IS IT?

Mind and mask are firmly established in the Universe of Brahman. Together in harmony, the two are closely connected to the reality.

The sages have said, the sky is established on the atmosphere, the atmosphere on the earth, the earth on the water, the water on the Reality and the Reality on Brahman which is the source of all. Reality does not originate. Brahman does not create. The world is a mystery. It can be understood as an aspect of the divine play (*lila*) in which the manifest comes from the unmanifest. God operates as a mask of Brahman. He assumes many forms, many names and many functions in his cosmic play. As a mask, he acts in the multilayered and multidimensional Reality which is independent of his potentiality or power. God, Animal and Man interchange and transpose their forms to play out the Self within. God's incarnation is an act of the cosmo-theandric play in which Animal and Man are used as mask. Mask is not 'false'; it reveals Reality. In modern scientific parlance, it is a 'virtual reality'. To a realized Man, the world itself is a mask for his soul.

The actor is not what appears from his act. In a theatrical performance, he wears a mask for his assigned role. The mask expresses the character that the actor plays on the arena. The audience is guided by the mask. The actor's performance is taken as reality where the actor is raised up to a state different from his normal self. As an artefact, the mask provides the actor a new identity, a new form, a new role, a new head. As a sacred object, it transforms the actor from Man to God. When an actor, for instance, plays the role of God (Rama, Krishna or Hanumana) his mind is temporarily elevated to that level of divinity. The audience also feels at the moment the vibration of divine forms. Mask as a form of the formless offers a divine knowledge that leads to enlightenment.

MIND AND MASK

The *Puranas* describe the miraculous birth of Ganesha from Parvati's peelings off. As soon as it was born, Parvati placed the child in Shiva's hands. To their surprise, the head of the young boy suddenly fell to the ground. A heavenly voice could then be heard, saying: 'You must choose a new head belonging to a being of superior quality'. Shiva then asked Nandi, the sacred bull, to set out. While on his search Nandi reached the paradise of Indra where he saw Airavata, Indra's white elephant, dozing. Nandi cut off Airavat's head and took it back to Shiva. To Parvati's joy, Shiva joined the elephant's head to his young son's body. Thereafter he was called Gajanan (the elephant-faced) and Bhavaputra (mind-born son). His divine body is described as having the elephant face with a single tusk, with the trunk curved, with a prominent belly, drooping ears, with a third eye. Smoke coloured, he is the awakened Spirit, the remover of obstacles. His consorts are Wisdom (*buddhi*) and Achievement (*siddhi*). He is initiator of all the arts, the bull among poets, the master of Yoga, the source and the soul of speech. He is known to have vanquished the demons of jealousy, vanity, delusion, anger, lust, egotism and arrogance. There is a story of the sage Vyasa who asked Ganesha to be the scribe of the great epic *Mahabharata* which he had just composed. Ganesha accepted on condition that the movement of his stylus on the palm leaves not be interrupted even once. Vyasa in his turn asked him not to record anything before understanding it perfectly. After having placed the sacred syllable *OM* on the top of his manuscript, Ganesha wrote the *Mahabharata*, the largest epic the world has ever known, at the speed of lightning.

The *pauranic* anthropology makes the elephant-faced God Ganapati as the First Mask symbolizing Mind and Nature. The components of intelligence, wisdom, brilliance, might and splendour are deep in his make-up. His vehicle, the Mouse, also symbolizes the features of Mind. A mouse by nature is aggressive, omnivorous, adaptable, fecund and resourceful. It is regarded as the master of the inside of everything. Every pervading self is a mouse which lives in the hole of intellect within the heart of every being. A mouse steals from people the things they enjoy and yet is not concerned whether those enjoyments are virtues or vices. Theft is the support of the immense being (Brahman), the essence of all names and shapes and yet remains hidden. Being the cause in all enjoyments he is the real enjoyer of pleasure. He is said to be a mouse. More fundamental is the integration of Being and Non-being in the domain of Mind.

WHO MASKS WHOM

If the Ganapati hypothesis is adopted, it will be reasonable to define all forms of life as components of a Mask of a single more complex system. Within the expanding Universe of Brahman, God, Animal and Man respond to Matter and Mind — the properties of life — and have the capacity to reproduce and grow into organizational structures. All the Three are motivated by purpose and their actions are directed towards some predetermined goals. Gods are self-born to create, to sustain and to destroy their own creation. When their cosmic goal is achieved, they die. This process is repeated. Life and Death are interdependent. Creation and Dissolution are a moving continuity. Life emerges from Death. Shiva, the God of Death, gives life to Ganapati to act as the scribe of the world history. The universal Mind makes Ganapati the Master of Yoga, the knowledge of uniting or yoking the fragmented aspects of reality.

Following the God Ganapati, masking the Mind of Man, with an animal face, is definitely the most appropriate step along the path of progressive complexification from Brahman Zero, God One, Animal Two and Man Three.

In the historically given factual world, the cosmic process of masking has great pragmatic consequences. There are two selves, qualitatively different: the higher and the lower, the spiritual and the natural and the useful and the erring. Masking involves the creation of a complete Self. It is a celebration or enactment of the creation of cosmos through the sacrifice of the Cosmic Man (*Purusa*). It is not just a means to vent human emotions in the usual artistic form.

In all traditional societies, ritual is the proper context of masking. Gods are formless; they assume anthropomorphic and zoomorphic forms. Humans have form; they assume transte-mporal powers by wearing the mask of God. Mask is the real representation of the God. While wearing the mask of a God, one 'becomes' that God. His own mind is switched off; he acquires a new mind and speaks through the mind of God. His personal consciousness is transformed into universal consciousness. In that state, he transcends the psychical and the physical. His human body does not prevent him from being one with the Mind of the whole Universe. He perceives no fissure in space-time. His memory moves into the past and the present; and he sees the future. He does not have the sense of his human identity. He is one with the God.

Mask has a face of two mysteries. There is the perspective of transcendence and there is the perspective of immanence. For traditional cultures, mask has both these perspectives. Even though the emphasis is on transcendence, the importance of aesthetic cognition is not denied.

THE MIND METAPHOR

Based on the revealed Truth, the Sacred Science presents a world-view and a language rich in metaphorical flow, integrating physical, psychical and spiritual levels of experience. It offers wide-ranging thoughts and allows us to think and live in a world suffused with meaning. In it, the metaphysical and physical are held in symbolic integration.

The mathematical sign we know as zero assigns to the subsuming concept the lack of an object. It is a kind of meta-sign that refers to the true and natural beginning. The equation of Mind as Brahman invoked the *real* reality. It brings us to a stage where Mind is inseparable from Matter and Matter inseparable from the Self.

The *upanisadic* science bestows upon Mind the ability to act as the inner controller, the universal Self. 'Mind is a bird tied to the breath of Life' and hence it is said: 'Beings are born from Mind, when born they live by Mind, on deceasing they enter into Mind'.

'Mind is the reins of the horses (senses) of a chariot (body)', which means Mind is the controlling power in relation to destiny and aspirations. So, it is said: 'The Mind alone is Man's cause of bondage and release'.

From the fact that Mind is of two kinds — pure and impure — there arises inevitably a certain kind of ignorance and a certain kind of helplessness with regard to man's behaviour. This is the major premise. The sages have drawn attention toward the distress of impure minds and the zeal for 'truth seeing' which pure mind alone can do. The medieval saint Kabir's metaphor of 'body as a pitch dark forest and Mind as an elephant gone mad' is a true analytical exploration of Mind, closed to the advance of psychological science.

The Ganapati hypothesis is the substitution of knowledge for ignorance and of reality for illusion (*Maya*). This makes it necessary to believe that Mind is a Mask which reveals as well as conceals.

The fluidity of Mind is accepted in tradition. The sages have prepared a unitary ground where the objective and subjective are included, but emphasis is given on the paramount source. As has been said:

> Speech is not what one should desire to understand.
> One should know the speaker.
> Smell is not what one should desire to understand.
> One should know the smeller.
> Form is not what one should desire to understand.
> One should know the seer.
> Sound is not what one should desire to understand.
> One should know the hearer.
> Taste is not what one should desire to understand.
> One should know the discerner of taste.
> The deed is not what one should desire to understand.
> One should know the doer.
> Pleasure and pain are not what one should desire to understand.
> One should know the discerner of pleasure and pain.
> Bliss, delight and procreation are not what one should desire to understand.
> One should know the discerner of bliss, delight and procreation.
> Going is not what one should desire to understand.
> One should know the goer.
> Mind is not what one should desire to understand.
> One should know the thinker.
>
> —*Kaushitaki Upanisada* 3.8

The chaos in the principle of psychology also refers to a purely fluid mind. But unlike the sages, the psychologists postulate, at the outset, the fact of thinking itself.

As a behavioural science, psychology is concerned with chaos in the inner and the outer realms. Chaotic behaviour contrasts with the ordered aspects of life or mind. But what may appear as a chaotic outside is not necessarily continuous with the inside. There is yet another dimension to be considered and that is the spiritual Mind. There are various types of ascetics, classified by the mystical state of their consciousness. The highest among them called *avadhuta* remains naked, eats like a cow, or lies down on his belly for eating, considers his body a corpse and makes no social distinction of any kind.

He is elevated to a higher state of pure consciousness (*turiya*). The outer chaos, or the absurdity of human existence, does not meddle with the blooming of spiritual consciousness.

During the nineteenth century, in order to differentiate between humans and animals, psychoanalysts claimed that animals lack in memory and learning, brain and neural complexity, reason and conceptual thought, language, culture, self-awareness, tool use, individual recognition, play and laughter and a sense of the future. In the seventeenth century western philosophy, animals have marked the divide between mortal beings — those capable of death — and 'automata' (Rene Descartes). In contrast, India's ancient sages made animals superior to humans and closest to Gods. In the beginning there were Deer-man, Frog-man, Tortoise-man who revealed the highest form of knowledge. Each God has an animal as a vehicle. Some animals have acquired the status of God. Animal metaphors are used to describe human wisdom, beauty and character. From ancient times to this day, this view is nourished by Indian philosophy and culture.

Chapter 7

The Cosmic Anthropological Principle

THE MANU PRINCIPLE

Indian tradition speaks of thought (or thinking about thought) as a transcendent phenomenon in the scheme of things. One of the earliest works on human organization is the *Manava Dharmashastra*, which literally means the 'Sacred Science of Man'. This text is the Word of *Manu*, the First Man. It reveals the cosmic anthropological principle, the Law of Life. Manu is the symbol of the universal consciousness which exists in the transcendent as also in the differentiated units of creation or in each individual centre which is but a ray from its source, the universal Sun. *Manu* is the Mind of the Creator, the principle of Ego. The Mind of the Creator is an ocean, of which the measure of Death is too profound to be known or comprehended by anyone. What Manu planned in his Mind, he executed it in his creation. There is a complete identity between the Creator and the Cosmos. *Manu* has a twofold aspect. He is above Time and Space and he is also the presiding ruler of each cosmic cluster of Time. Each *Manu* is the sovereign ruler of his dynastic Time and it is in his charge that the primeval ordinance be fully and perfectly fulfilled in his period. It is the Manu-principle that governs the Indian vision of science and society.

There is another principle which touches on a crucial problem that could easily be the starting point for understanding Man and his Universe. It is the Matter-principle that elucidates the fundamental elements in their gross and subtle aspects of reality. The third is the Creating-principle, which throws light on the cause and the ultimate basis of the world. These three interrelated principles are set in motion from the very beginning of the world. The vision of the Sacred Science proceeds from the primordial source of knowledge, which is infinite; it is continually transmitted to this world to the extent that Man has not ceased to read the signs.

The conceptual categories of the Sacred Science discourses merge into a unity of thought, quite different from the anthropological concept of binary opposites.

ONE AS MANY

The *upanisadic* sages had described Brahman as *bindu*, the dimensionless point, literally a drop. The *bindu* consists of the unity of two: one static and the other dynamic. It is the dynamic aspect that expresses itself as the Universe of multiplicity, but it essentially remains One, the epitome of all. In geometry the point is the Sun, that is, the centre with a circumference. There is a centre and a periphery, diameter and radius. The circle is a point expanded: the meeting of four equal lines forms a square and three lines come together to form a triangle. These primary forms are fundamental to Hindu thought.

The concept of *sunya* (zero), when applied to Brahman, the Absolute, is unthinkable in itself. Metaphysically it is identified with both fullness and emptiness. The description of Brahman as full and empty, shows that it is beyond the dialectical opposites of time and timelessness, formed and unformed, mortal and immortal, actual and beyond; and so on. The whole Universe is regarded as a living organism. The Golden Germ is a cosmic metaphor attributed to the origin of the Universe. Here gold symbolizes the principle of light shining forth from within the womb of darkness. The sap within the Egg originally existed in an undifferentiated form but later were born the seven primeval ancestors, or seven differentiated life forces (Mind, Life and the Five Elements of Matter). The Egg floated in Water for thousand years and then something triggered it off. It split into two and the whole Universe came into existence.

The organic units of the Universe are further clarified by an anthropic metaphor. From the limbs of *Purusa*, the Cosmic Man, everything originated: strophes and melodies, horses and every animal, the four human castes, the Sky, the Atmosphere, the Ocean, the Earth, the Moon, the Sun, the Fire, the Wind and the King of Gods. The idea of organic relationship is pursued to a high degree of sophistication.

The geometric description highlights the plurality of primary forms: the square, the circle and the triangle. In the description of the Cosmic Egg or Man, the One is not the all, that is, the One is not the sum total; the One subsists in the many. Although the world of plurality has emerged out of the One, the One is not affected by the defects of the many. Here, the One is to be understood as a dimension of the Self. The primordial oneness arises from within the Self. Hence it makes differentiation possible. The individual Self is valuable precisely because all generic and ontic differences are included in the One, the universal Self.

MAN AS MICROCOSM

Anthropologists' conception of Man is grounded in the theory of evolution. In biology, evolution refers to slow changes in the process of growth. Applied to human evolution, it implies that Man represents the pinnacle of evolution and his world is pinned to a ladder of progressive development. Today, evolutionists and creationists are in the midst of a continuous ideological struggle. The supporters of 'scientific creationism', which developed in America in the early 1970s, say the following: evolution and creation are competing scientific models. Since evolution is merely a model and is not testable by experimentation, one must have faith that it is true. If an alternative model for Nature would correlate the facts better than the evolution model, then it would be the one to believe.

There is another theory which looks inward upon Man and the Universe. Its basic assumption is that like the rest of the material world, Man's body is made up of the Five Primordial Elements: Earth, Water, Fire, Air and Sky. Each major organ is said to have its own builder. Head and ears are associated with Sky, neck and chest with Air, stomach with Fire and body with Earth. The five fingers, from the little finger to the thumb, are associated with Earth, Water, Fire, Air and Sky, respectively. Elements are also known to have caused the origin of bio-social types. For example, blacksmiths relate themselves with Earth, carpenters with Water, coppersmiths with Fire, sculptors with Air and goldsmiths with Sky.

The theory of the Five Elements leaps forward to the vision of the Five 'sheaths' or envelopes: (i) the gross body or the vegetative envelope; (ii) the vital body; (iii) the mental body; (iv) the poetic or higher intellectual envelope; and (v) the beatific envelope, which is the highest in the realization of self-knowledge and self-control.

Man's relationship with the Universe is explained by a powerful imagery of the Cosmic Man, with thousand heads, thousand eyes and thousand feet, encompassing the planet Earth on all sides and exceeding it by ten fingers' breath. This does not make the world anthropocentric. The Cosmic Man is neither being nor non-being. From him the shining Cosmic Egg was born and from this again he himself emerged. In other words, he became the creature of his own creation. From this creature, the four human classes (*varnas*) took birth. All creatures emanating from the cosmic body are invested with cosmic powers and functions.

Clearly, this perception of Man as microcosm is different from what evolutionism and creationism claim.

SCIENCE AS SOCIETY

The Manu-principle connects biology with cosmology. All life operates at the level of existence. Life and Death together form a continuum. All contingent beings originate from Space and to Space they return. Movement is a feature common to all beings. What moves is the individual Self, not the body. What dissolves is the body, not the Self. With this idea came the notion of human deeds and reincarnation.

The process by which man-woman, husband-wife, sprang relates to a cosmological principle. The One was the size of a man and a woman in close embrace. It split (*pat*) into two and from that arose husband (*pati*) and wife (*patni*). Hence it is said: oneself is like half a potsherd. Husband and wife are indissolubly united. This has been expressed in several ways. Whatever the qualities of the man with whom a woman is united according to the Law, such qualities even she assumes, like a river united with the ocean.

He only is a perfect man who consists of the three persons united: his wife, himself and his offspring. The theory of heredity is proclaimed. The woman is the soil and the man is the seed. The production of all corporeal beings takes place through the union of the soil with the seed. In some cases, the seed is more distinguished and in some the womb of the female; but when the two are equal, the offspring is most highly esteemed. On comparing the seed and the receptacle of the seed, the seed is declared to be more important; for the offspring of all created beings is marked by the characteristics of the seed.

The parent-child unity has been conceptualized in its genetic and spiritual oneness. As has been said: 'You move into the womb of Prajapati (the Father of all creatures). You yourself are born again'. The continuity of the Self conveys still another, though related, message. A child has two births even before he is actually born: the first in the state of the seed in the father and the second in which it enters the womb of the mother. The beauty of the relationship of the Self can be appreciated in this organized reasoning: 'He (the son) who is one self of his (father) is made his substitute (in the world) for (the performance of) meritorious deeds. Then the other self of his (father) having done his duties, enters old age and departs. He, as soon as departs from here, is born again. This is his (son's) third birth'.

The parent and the child form a continuity of the Self; and the husband, the wife and the offspring, a perfect unit. The unity is maintained in the lifetime and beyond Time (that is, even after Death) by performing the ancestral rites. 'The parent, being nourisher, should be nourished' is the ordinance.

Kinship does not remain a mere social relation between two living persons; it is the human energy conserved through generations. Kinship in this life may be much more complicated, but its continuity in the other world does not conflict with the fundamental laws of energy. The law of conservation of energy is as true for Life as for Matter.

The Cosmic Principle of the One makes a complete sense in the fourfoldness of human organization. The imagery of the fourfold *varna* as the limbs (mouth, arms, legs, feet) of the Cosmic Man involves essentially an organic relationship. Each *varna* is a member of the personal aspect of the whole of reality. A *varna* is more than the sum total of all individuals: it subsists in many.

Human beings are classified into four categories, each *varna* being ordained to pursue a specific, hereditary, non-competitive occupation so as to ensure harmony and prosperity of the Universe. This is comprehended along a line of continuum.

Human life is ordered into four stages. The life of a Brahmana or a Kshatriya starts with learning and spiritual disciplining, rises to the culmination of worldly prosperity, retreats to the forest from where they had begun their intellectual journey and finally forsakes all possessions and worldly emotional entanglement. The wholeness of life is maintained by performing evenly balanced roles at different stages. This scheme tallies with the Cosmic Law of return to the primordial. In the operational context of human organization, the system eliminates all possibility of generation gap.

Human desires are also classified into four categories: the desire for righteousness in the sense of duty, the desire connected with wealth, the desire for pleasure and procreation and the desire for transcending all desires. The fulfilment of the fourfold desire is the approved goal of life. Although opposing in character, these desires stand in an organic and interactive relationship to one another; in effect they are counterpoised. The desire for 'wealth' and pleasure must be fulfilled, but strictly in accordance with the sense of duty. And the desire for the fulfilment of worldly duty must give way to liberation. This arrangement helps every individual feel satisfied and contented with the freedom and fullness of Life. It completes the cosmic rhythm and forms a single continuum of inward and outward.

THEODICY AS COSMODICY

Christian theology considers Man as a special creation set apart from the rest of the animal kingdom which has been created to serve his needs and pleasure.

Animals have no share in salvation and no position in eternity. Supporting the Christian theological explanation, Descartes reasoned that there was a qualitative and unbridgeable barrier between Man and Animal. Charles Darwin took an antithetical view, as he brought up the subject of the origin and evolution of life on Earth. He claimed to have proved in his theory that no essential difference separated Man from other animals. The modern post-Christian West has overcome the two extremes by saying that Man is an animal but a very peculiar one and in many ways a unique animal. His uniqueness lies in his capacity for conceptual thinking, his cumulative tradition, his tools and his speech. Of his biological peculiarities, he is by far the most variable wild species, a dominant type and unique in the method of his evolution.

Cultures differ in their self-evaluation and understanding of the other. Most cultures have traditionally maintained that a powerful bond exists between God (Spirit), Man and Animal. No one occupies a special place in the scheme of the Universe. No one is unique. All creatures have a completely cosmic origin in the self-designed Universe. One exists in relation to the other. All are subject to the eternal cycle of birth and death. The Cosmic Law has no beginning, no end. It is boundless, but what comes out from the boundless is bounded. Thus it turns out that, technically speaking, all are 'reincarnated beings'.

The Hindus are antithetical of creationism and even more of evolutionism, but are not opposed to the spirit of science in its original sense (*sapientia*). The picture of the Universe is painted as an expanding Brahman with a centre. The first three (God, Animal and Man) form a divine triangle on the surface of the Universe. They are the chief actors of this great theatre. Ocean cosmology links all of them in a remarkable way. The Cosmic Egg that lay within the 'womb' was the light of Brahman, which is visible to us as Life. The auto-fission of the One (Cosmic Egg) caused the many. God Vishnu took incarnations. Of his ten complete incarnations, the first three were animal forms, the fourth was a composite form (animal-man), the fifth was a dwarf and the next four were fully developed humans.

Animals are not only the earliest forms but also the most variable species living in varied ecological conditions of Water, Earth and Sky. Practically all conceivable forms of animals are associated with the Hindu pantheon—some as incarnations of God and others as God's vehicles. Each form is divine and unique in its genetic character and behavioural qualities. As God has assumed the powers of Brahman, so have animals derived God's qualities and powers. Animals seem to have set standards for Man: in productive power; in swiftness, energy and strength; in mien and courage; in docility and inoffensiveness; in self-sacrificing quality; in artistic manifestation and beauty; in intelligence and faith; and so on. Ontological change in the moral order of time follows the degrees of respect for animals. Man is also a virtual animal (*pashu*, the 'roped' one). So are the Gods because they are also 'roped' by the cycle of life and death. Hindu astrology makes Man intrinsically inseparable from Animal. Every human being has two births, one from a human mother and another from a female animal, depending on the asterism at birth.

God, Animal and Man are not seen in terms of phylogeny. There is no path of evolution, no selection and no survival of the fittest. No species develop out of other species. The number of species is fixed. Each species is unique in itself. Eschatology provides the idea of inter-species biological connection outside Time, in no Time. It is the Soul, the life-force, that switches from one form to another. Animal 'ancestors' (totems) play a decisive role in social life and ritual. Both God and Man may enter into animal species in their next births. The fortune of Men and of Gods is believed to be in the Animal. God and Man live in mystical symbiosis with the animal world. Their purpose of existence is to maintain the original symmetry of the two worlds to which God provides super-symmetry.

MIND AS COSMOS

For modern science, Mind is a mere biological organism and has a purely physical basis. The Sacred Science offers a richer and more encompassing view of reality that in the beginning there was only Mind. Mind created the Word. Word created the Life-Breath. Beings are born from Mind, when born they live by Mind and after death they enter into Mind. The body consists of Mind. Mind is the agent in all conscious experience. Mind is the formless Matter. He who dwells in the Mind, is yet other than Mind, whom the Mind does not know, whose body is the Mind, who controls the Mind from within—He is the Self within you, the Inner Controller, the Immortal. It is at this level of thought that Mind is inseparable from Matter, Matter inseparable from Life and Life inseparable from the universal Self.

Mind is of two kinds: pure and impure. It becomes impure when it is touched by desire and pure when it is freed from desire. When a Man, having made his mind perfectly stable, free from attachment and confusion, enters upon the 'mindless state', he attains the supreme abode. The Mind alone is Man's cause of bondage or release; it leads to bondage when attached to the sense objects and it leads to release when free from them.

Psychology is concerned with chaos in inner and outer realms. Chaotic behaviour contrasts with the ordered aspects of Life or Mind. There is another dimension to be considered and that is the spiritual Mind. An ascetic, at the mystical state of his consciousness, remains naked, eats like a cow or lies down on his belly for eating, considers his body a corpse and makes no social distinction of any kind. He is elevated to a higher state of pure consciousness. The outer chaos, or the absurdity of human existence, does not meddle with the blooming of his spiritual consciousness. At another level, Mind is both Cosmos and Chaos. Man participates in the mystery of cosmodicy/theodicy. Anthropodicy is inconceivable.

WORD AS WORLD

Tradition tells us in innumerable ways that Word is World. The Word, imperishable, is the First born of Truth. The Word is infinite and immense. All the Gods, the celestial spirits, Men and Animals, live in the World. In the Word all the worlds find their support. The Veda is not the Word of God. Nor is it inspired or authored by God. It is simply the primordial Word of which no human being is the author. This Word is the consort of the creator of the world. She was at the beginning. She is the source of human knowledge. She is the primordial mystery combining in herself the three worlds of Time: past, present and future. No wonder then, every Word is sacred and powerful.

The ultimate reality is of the nature of 'Word-principle' and from it are manifested all the objects of the world, the whole cosmos. The Word has been measured out in four degrees, three kept hidden; Men speak only the fourth degree of wisdom.

There are three aspects of the Word, three states through which it passes whenever one speaks; that is, when the Word, which is at first internal, is externalized for the purpose of communication: (a) *vaikhari*, the intoned Word, the most external stage when it is uttered by the speaker and heard by the hearer; (b) *madhyama*, the middle one, going inward, the stage associated chiefly with the Mind, the intellect and not with the organs of articulation; and (c) *pashyanti*, the seeing one, the innermost stage, which is said to have infinite varieties. It is also described as being of a lower and a higher kind. The higher kind is beyond the range of verbal usage; it is the highest dimension of the Word. Potentially, (a) could leap into (b) and (b) to (c). More correctly, there is a logical continuity between the levels of (a) and (b). At the level of (c) discontinuity begins. Also, (c) is doubly discontinues with reference to (a) and (b) and with reference to the highest dimension of the Word. In the (b) stage there is no actual split or succession in the Word. The stage (c) is aware of itself. *Para*, the higher stage, is beyond such self-awareness. Or the self-awareness of the higher stage is (c).

Word as expressible experience, originates in the 'twilight language' of the non-manifest. To communicate their experience of 'seeing the Word', the saints have developed a language of 'light-and-darkness'—partly light, partly darkness. It is also called the language of the 'inverted flute', the enigmatic 'turned around' language. The sound of the 'inverted flute' is silence that measures the trace of what is in itself immeasurable. Kabir describes the power of the 'spoken' Word: 'In the one Word are thirty-six melodies; it makes the music infinite. God is the Letterless One'.

KNOWLEDGE AS EXPERIENCE

As part of the modern systems of knowledge, anthropology prides itself in being *autotelic*, that is, human thought ought to be pursued for its own sake. This claim is consistent with the general theory of human evolution that makes Man the *telos* of his own thoughts, works and deeds. Man makes himself and his own history and civilization by virtue of his rational powers. He alone is the possessor of knowledge and the conqueror of Nature.

In the Indian theory of knowledge, the key concept is 'Cosmic Intelligence', which sustains the life-force and vigour of all that exists. This divinity cannot be 'known', if by knowledge one understands a merely mental consciousness. It can be approached only by sacrifice, by holy action and by other means of entering into the 'womb' of the Ultimate. In other words, the primal knowledge is self-existent. At the human level it designates the cosmic process of knowing and also the result of it (acquired knowledge).

The other dimensions are: critical knowledge up to analytical consciousness, right knowledge, knowledge of the ultimate Reality (the total realization), knowledge of 'objective' Reality or true knowledge and wisdom, or full consciousness. These categories stress a certain type of global knowledge. There is another set of concepts that emphasizes the type of more detailed and rational knowledge, vision and perception. The third set relates to thinking, the process of knowing. The fourth group represents the world-view, the systematic vision of Reality, intellectual perception, dream, mirror and doctrinal systems.

A mystical process of knowing the unknowable is reported from all traditional cultures. The process of experiencing is not just knowing; it means becoming a part of the experienced object. By experience one understands immediate contact with the real. In the perfect experience there would be no difference between the experiencing subject and the experiencing object. Experience is untransferable and personal. It is said that the knower of the Ultimate becomes speechless. What this implies is, coming into direct contact with the source of knowledge, Man is elevated to a state of primordial consciousness where the knowable merges with the unknowable. There is much to do in this field: the 'anthropology of experience'.

KNOWLEDGE AS CULTURE

Culture may be conceived of as a deposit of knowledge accumulated in space-time. The deposit of each culture is made up of two parts: 'manifest' and 'unmanifest'. The manifest part contains the knowledge of things revealed and discovered. The unmanifest part contains the beliefs and hopes of what is yet to be revealed and discovered. Revelation and discovery keep the manifest part of the deposit in a state of flux; the unmanifest part remains in a perpetual state of mystification. Thus any classification of culture based on mere empirical content (that is, the manifest part) is bound to be partial and tentative. A relatively enduring and valid classification can be sought in terms of the modes of transmission of knowledge. There are three modes of transmission: oral (*laukika*), textual (*shastriya*) and transcendental (*naivrittika*), each forming an organic unity of thought and action. Accordingly, there are Oral, Textual and Transcendental cultures.

Based upon personal factors in the development of thought, cultures are fourfold: (i) Cosmocentric culture, which recognizes the vital significance of Cosmic Elements in the making of biological and cultural Man. (ii) Theocentric culture, which considers dissociation from the phenomenal world in favour of the divine eternal world as human perfection. (iii) Anthropocentric culture, which makes Man the measure of all and teaches a path to progress which is external to Nature. (iv) Technocentric culture, which worships technology in the belief and hope that higher possibilities of Man lie in affluence (temporal power), which is largely and necessarily a function of advancing technology. Of these, the first two types maintain that life and culture originate dependently in the total context of divine Nature, which is changing and yet not changing. The path of human perfection lies within it: Man in harmony with Nature. In the other two types, there is a constructed environment unconnected with Nature, where the systems of Man and that of the machine are in conflict.

NATURE AS CULTURE

The Newtonian view of Nature as a vast machine and the Darwinian conception of Nature as an evolutionary process remain deeply ingrained in western thought and culture. Both involve some form of antithesis between the purely physical and the animate. In the former, it is a stark dichotomy between Matter and Mind; in the latter, it is the persistent contrast of organism to environment. The outcome is a 'culture of power and wealth', embodying the forces of colonization and 'ladder mentality'. Although the new physics and the new biology in our times have gone far beyond the old notions of materialism and evolutionism, there appears no concomitant change in the scientist's basic attitude towards Nature and culture.

There is another perception: Man *in* Nature. He sees Nature as his own self in becoming. He is moulded and engendered by Nature. Man *and* Nature, Nature *and* Mind, Matter *and* Mind and Body *and* Mind are fused into a single reality. Man as Soul or Spirit is the Cosmic Person, as a body he is the non-sentient Nature. Together as world systems they are the primal 'seed' and 'womb' for all human cultures.

The existential connection between Nature and culture is explained: Elements of Nature are by themselves inert and incapable of self-movement; they move only by an extraneous agent, the Spirit. All living matter exists by the transcendent Order of Life, the one which is invisible, formless, but knowable through its effect. It renders matter the binding abilities, interlocking powers, overlapping characters and a transcendent state in which Nature is seen as a self-originating, self-organizing and self-sustaining system. Nobody knows where that Order comes from but it is seen all around. Nature nurtures the Element. The whole process of growth and decay, order and disorder, may be seen in the rhythm of night and day or the cycle of the seasons and in Space and Time. At the human level, it causes bio-social types, as in the Hindu caste system (based on the principle of the genetic algorithm).

Like Elements of Nature, the forms of culture are also subject to a fivefold order of origination, binding, interlocking, overlapping and transcending. The biological Man, made of Elements, is ritually processed as a social person. The social person undergoes a transcendent (supernatural, super-psychic) process of cultivation and purification to become a cultural person. The ultimate goal of human life is transcendence, that is, the ordering of desires of earthly existence. Human desires are fourfold: desire to uphold the natural order, the desire connected with the sustenance of Life, the desire for bringing oneself into existence (by the natural process of reproduction) and the desire of transcending all desires. This approach to Life and culture is a deeply religious one. In a consciously cultivated lifestyle, directed towards the boundless dimension of naturalness, Man as Nature is enlightened. The non-homocentric and non-technocentric view of culture takes Man as a member of the class of 'sentient being', or even as 'non-sentient being' and therefore the image of the Cosmic Man. When it is said that Man has a kinship with trees and animals, the cosmological emphasis is quite conspicuous.

Drawing upon the *upanishadic* imagery of the *ficus religiosa* tree, culture may be defined as an 'inverted tree' with roots in the revealed, imperishable tradition, whose stem is represented by the ritual process of transformation, whose tender leaves are the various stages of life and whose branches are the social groups nourished by action (with or without attraction and repulsion). This tree extends both downwards in earthly existence and upwards in the transcendental realm.

The true nature of human culture is imperceptible. It has neither a beginning nor an end (that is, it is ahistorical and its source is the Cosmic Intelligence), nor even stability (that is, perennial flow of tradition). Its roots are so deep-laid in transcendence that it cannot be cut by the temporal weapons of destruction (technology). From this tree has emanated a pattern of life freed from the pairs of opposites: pleasure and pain, sacred and profane, inner and outer; and so on.

RITUAL AS LANGUAGE

Of all the animals, Man alone speaks a language other than his own. He communicates with birds and beasts. He also communicates with Gods, spirits and ancestors. He has learnt a ritual way of communication, the language of the God. Ritual is always a code which points to something beyond, that which cannot be expressed in human language. In its essential form it is a fourfold code consisting of (i) primordial Word, (ii) gesture, (iii) sound and (iv) everyday language. The primordial Word used in ritual is that of which neither Man nor God is the author. It is not even the message of the God. Indeed, it is God himself. There are innumerable gestures with positions of body, hands and fingers. A gesture is sometime performed by pronouncing a primordial Word, generally for the fruition of the Word. Sound is the third constituent of the ritual language. As in outer space, waves of sound are produced by movements of air, so in the space within the body, waves of sound are produced according to the movements of the vital air and the process of inhalation and exhalation. Certain forms of sound are considered sacred and auspicious. There are also inauspicious sounds such as the hooting of an owl or the howl of a dog or a jackal. In all forms of chants and recitations, the critical aspect is sound. The fourth constituent of the ritual code is the use of everyday language.

Ritual as a human phenomenon, displaying different dimensions of the relationship between Man and language, is universal. Since man's desire to know his place in the Universe and to overcome his existential crisis is universal, ritual language is found in all cultures. Each culture constructs its own world of the sacred. The forms of ritual language, therefore, vary from one culture to another. But the basic fourfold code suggested here is applicable to all cultures and to all kinds of religious expression. Ritual is an internal necessity. It has a function and relevance for Man because it determines his subconscious activities and gives the noblest expression of his life and culture. For a man in tradition, tradition has an authority above which no authority exists.

TRADITION AS HIERO-HISTORY

Tradition perceived as hiero-history refers to time in which every-time is restored to the present. Here restoration of time is not to be understood as bringing back to the original state; it means a continual renaissance. The nearest Sanskrit word for tradition is *parampara* (one after another) which signifies layers of precipitated matter accumulated in Time, as in a flood and refers to a deposit of knowledge to be nourished and to be handed down to posterity. Man is creator only in a limited sense. The basic structure of the tradition that has been revealed to him is 'unlimited in extent and unequalled in authority'. His own job is to explore, to discover and to rediscover the 'unlimited' treasure that has been handed down to him through a series of revelations. This, of course, he does in numerous ways.

The process of intellectualization of tradition is neither so simple nor so frequent as to be brought about in everyday life. Tradition-making is based on the truth-abiding principle, on the rigours of intellectual exercise. It passes through a fivefold consideration of: (i) competence, (ii) criteria of truth, (iii) fullness, (iv) compelling situation and (v) purification. Of these, the first three are procreative and the last two restorative in purpose and performance.

The norms and values of traditional society are governed by the Law of Limits to change. Tradition, by definition, is changeable. Change occurs inevitably in handing down the deposit of knowledge from one generation to the next. In a certain sense, each generation organizes its own tradition in a manner which may differ slightly or sharply from the preceding generations, as also from the generations to come. But change is brought about necessarily within certain limits defined by the tradition. In this manner each generation, while experiencing the present, is continuous with the past and with the future. For cultures believing in the cyclic concept of time, chronological ordering of tradition is not only unimportant but also logically inconsistent. Additions and omissions in scriptures really do not matter so long as tradition is considered in its fullness. As the sages have said, 'From fullness fullness take away; fullness yet remains'.

Tradition as excellence of human organization is threefold: contextualized convention, conventionalized universal and universalized transcendence. Human life is modelled by practical experience made intelligible by conventional universal experience, authenticated by the criteria of truth. Each generation contextualizes conventional experience in order to make it intelligible, recognizable and operationally viable. In time its contextualized experience becomes the conventionalized universal experience for the next generation. Backward in time are the roots of human experience—the revealed universalized transcendence—shared by every generation.

It follows, then, that ordinarily at no point of time can tradition be fully realized; it can be realized only in proportion to its intelligibility. Tradition in its fullness remains timeless. But this timelessness is not to be taken as that of the pure transcendence because it consists in a co-ordination between empirical knowledge and revelatory knowledge. It may be viewed as a certain mixture of the temporal and the transcendental reality.

UNIFICATION PRINCIPLE

The western science of man seeks to understand Man empirically by an analysis and comparison of different races and cultures. Its theory appeared to be impregnable so long as it was confined to the 'garden' of simple folk. The shift from simple to complex cultures with a high intellectual tradition has posed a big challenge. This brings us to a methodic consideration that introduces the premises of cosmic unification on which traditional cultures stand. Modern cultures have other premises.

All traditional cultures hold that different human groups form, as it were, different life-centres originating from a cosmic condition and influencing one another in a given context of space-time, that is, cosmology is seen a complete set of basic laws of culture. Needless to say that this vision has startling implications for anthropology, particularly that of the old style which supposes that a single culture (i.e. the modern technocentric culture) can set standards for determining the state of all cultures.

The key concept in the Sacred Science of Man is Brahman, the mystery of cosmodicy. The word Brahman has acquired a series of technical meanings, out of which has evolved the metaphysical Brahman, in its manifold forms. It has been identified and interpreted as the potency or principle from which all things are derived, as the ultimate basis of the world, as the inner power and essence of things, as the unity of all that is named, as the form of Time and the refuge of all beings, as the fire, the wind, the lightning, the heart or the breath of life, speech, sight, hearing, understanding; and so on. With reference to the person, the Mind is Brahman, with reference to the divinities, Space. Among Gods (Brahma and others) Brahman appeared by means of Agni (Fire) and among men as a Brahmana.

Of the fourfold *varna*, the Brahmana is more 'powerful' than the other three. According to Manu, the very birth of a Brahmana is an internal incarnation of the *dharma*. The epics often repeat that 'The Brahmana is the highest *tejas* (power, energy); the Brahmana is the highest *tapas* (power of asceticism); it is by the honouring of Brahmanas that the Sun shines in the Sky; having prowess, consisting in truth and gifted with great energy, such men, if enraged, are capable of reducing the entire kingdom to ashes; and so on'. The *varna* order was extended beyond the world of Men. Of the four kinds of soil, the Brahmana soil is white in colour; of the temples the Brahmana form is characterized by nine divisions of the wall; of the planets, Jupiter and Venus are Brahmana; of the signs of the zodiac, Pisces, Scorpio and Taurus are Brahmana. According to Hindu astrology, every individual, regardless of his being a Brahmana, a Kshatriya, a Vaishya or a Shudra by birth, has a *varna* of his own which is determined by the sign of the zodiac at the time of his birth. Thus there is a chance for every individual to be a Brahmana. The fourfold *varna* order pervaded also the plant and animal kingdoms. Among animals, the cow is Brahmana and among trees, the banyan is Brahmana.

The identity of the Brahmana as *varna*, the Brahma as creator and the Brahman as the Universe is clearly borne out by the divine precepts. The idea that Gods, humans, animals and trees are recipients of the 'divine power' is not confined to India. Like the Indian Brahman, the Siouan term *Wakan* indicates a wonderful power with which the Universe is believed to be charged; and just like Brahman, *Wakan* may be a formula or a place or an object or a person. The Kwakiutl term *Nawalak* has a very wide range of meaning (e.g. trees, the lark, the salmon, supernatural beings that manifest in visions, persons celebrating or joining religious ceremonies, etc.). The Munda term *Bonga* refers to a very big power that pervades the Universe and, though being formless by itself, can assume any form. Among the Suau-Tawala (Papua), the term *Gigibori* applies not only to 'power' but also to things and persons in which this 'power' resides. The Polynesian term *mana* also stands with the 'power' concept. Each of these terms or concepts has specific characteristics of its own. But the fact that Brahman is a central concept among a large number of concepts cannot be denied. All that is connected with such a 'power-concept' can, in principle, bear the name 'Cosmic hierophany'. Our cosmic hierophany (= a nearly self-sufficient partial modality of manifestation) is earth-bound and ruled by Death. But there are other cosmic hierophanies (= an ordered and pre-eminent modality of the plenum — the great chain of Being) which are not earth-bound. The personal and the impersonal, the animate and the inanimate, the human and the divine and the divine and the cosmic get entirely intermingled or unified in the manifest aspect of the potency called Brahman.

This aspect of the Cosmic hierophany is closely bound up with the solving of the anthropologists' riddle of binary opposites. The sages have described Brahman as *coincidentia oppositorum*.

ECOLOGICAL PRINCIPLE

The manifested cosmoses are spatio-temporal and have immensely long life. They are earth-bound but spiritually alive in the domain of Brahman.

The Five Elements of our world have been perceived holistically as symbols standing for the ultimate constituent of Reality. The Elements are both material and spiritual. What binds them together is the Soul, the Inner Controller.

Man, whose body is made of the Elements, does not know who dwells in these Elements. The sages have said that the Earth is the Mother, the Sky is the Father; the Waters, the Fire and the Air convey the divine energy. Human existence is given over to spiritual kinship with Nature.

Man's attitude towards the planet Earth springs from his primordial experience. The Earth is his home, his own family, his body. He finds his happiness on the Earth. He discovers an intelligent pattern of understanding. The Earth is a cosmic power, the protector of all creatures. The imagery of Mother Earth is extended to a new symbol. Universal Nature or infinity has been conceived as the wish-fulfilling Cosmic Cow in whose body all the divine powers abide. The Earth is her milking-pail. This Cow has four udders for streams of milk by which she supports four classes of creature: the sages, the ancestors, the Gods and the men. What amazing wisdom is embodied in this belief is that the Earth has inexhaustible resources, enough for the survival of all.

For the sages, ecology was the Sacred Science from which they worked out a cultural formulation to realize that all life on Earth is valuable, not just the life of *Homo sapiens*. They also made Man aware of the cosmic gift, bringing confidence and happiness to human life. Tragically, the modern Man is ambivalent towards his relationship with the Earth. In Christian thinking this ambivalence has pervaded through the two thousand years of the Christian story.

Man cannot live without the Earth. At the same time, he is more than Earth. As the limb of the Cosmic Man, he is mighty. As a microcosm, his body is made of Cosmic Elements and his Self (Soul) is enveloped by the Cosmic sheaths. From the primordial sacrifice he emerged as a ritual being. He is both a biological creature and a spiritual being: hence an autonomous being, partly free.

Man is conditioned by the Law of Life. But he is capable of the existential leap that takes him to another reality. The Buddhist theory of 'dependent origination' explains how an individual life passes through birth upon birth in the form of consciousness and how by the same chain of causation, the wheel of Life stops for ever. Man's existence in the cosmic realm cannot be fully comprehended without taking into account his relationship with other beings and non-beings. The implication is that neither in *sansara* (cyclic flow of birth-death) nor in *nirvana* (cessation of rebirth) is Man alone and unique. In a general ultimate sense, he, as a species, cannot attain *nirvana* until all beings and non-beings are fully enlightened. This idea is well developed in the Mahayanist tradition, which holds that animals, birds, trees, mountains, rivers and lands too attain Buddhahood. The interchange between human and cosmic is reflected further in the concept of the three kinds of body: (i) the body with human form; (ii) the body without any form or substratum, subtle and eternal; and (iii) the body made of Mind. Of these, the eye of the flesh can see the human body and not the other two, which can be seen only by the Divine. The eternal body of the Buddha persists through space and time; it assumes form in various ways. Similarly, the human body can be transformed in many spiritual ways.

This is the most remarkable explanation of the relationship between the physical and spiritual dimensions of Man. In witnessing the plunder of the Earth in many countries today, the notion of Mother Earth and the Cosmic Cow is not only a revelation of the self-perpetuating life process of the Earth but also a hope and message, the spiritual transformation of Man and his world.

ORDERING PRINCIPLE

Traditional cultures refer to a fivefold Cosmic Order that sets forth the timeless sequence of creation, preservation and dissolution. The First Order is set in zero, that is, in the beginning there was nothing. The Second Order causes primary creation of the five Cosmic Elements. The Third Order causes natural identity and differentiation in terms of colour, direction, form, smell, etc. The Fourth Order causes the return to the primordial state. The Fifth Order is the Order of all orders. It repeats the scenario of the world in which everything has its proper place and where everything grows and allows others to grow. It is inviolable.

The Cosmic Order plunges into the Human Order. Traditional societies are structured on a fourfold order in terms of their social formation, subsistence, distinctions and desires. Human groups are ordered by three *gunas* (factors of quality), called *sattva* (light, intelligence), *rajas* (energetic, active, domineering) and *tamas* (coarse, inert, enveloping, dark). Nature is also constituted of these factors of quality. Combining in various proportions, they make up the evolving Universe. Hence the potential differences between individuals and the objects of the Universe. In the hierarchical order, *sattva* is placed at the top because it is luminous and contrasted with *tamas*, which is the lowest. All physical and mental phenomena are placed under the hierarchy of the three factors. In the human world those who possess *sattva* in abundance are called Brahmana, those with *rajas* are Kshatriya and those with *tamas* are Vaishya or Shudra.

All Orders are subjected to the Law of Numbers. The number possesses an active force. It is a symbol and its properties are sacred attributes. Like the divisions of Time, numbers are divine for a similar reason. They are said to have been revealed to mankind by the motions of the stars. They play a unique privileged role in determining the hierarchy of infinite sets which are incomprehensible or else chaotic. The numbers are formulated in terms of cultural symbols and have possibly pre-mathematical existence. For instance, in Indian thought, Three signifies states of Elements, Gods, Vedas, factors of quality, etc.; Four signifies Ages, castes of Men, stages of life, kinds of creation, kinds of creature, etc.; Five signifies primordial Elements, faces of God, cosmic sheaths, classes of sages, etc.; Seven signifies seas, mountains, planets, streams of the River Ganga, divisions of the stratosphere, attendants of the Sun, etc. Clearly, the number illuminates the relation of signs to meta-signs. Zero, understood as a number, assigns to the subsuming concept of the Absolute or the Ultimate—it is full and empty.

There are two forms of Brahman: the formed and the formless, the mortal and the immortal, the stationary and the moving. Similarly, there are two types of humans. The one whose thought is individually formed is mortal and moving, the other who believes in formless is immortal and stationary. So are two orders of culture: the New and the Old. The New Order is formed on the premise that Man is the measure of all and hence can create, destroy and recreate the world at his will; that human thought ought to be pursued for its own sake and that the new system of knowledge is 'autotelic'. The Old Order maintains that the primal culture moves and it moves not. In using the *upanishadic* metaphor, it can be said that traditional cultures have historically moved in time and yet its critical intuition of understanding the Reality remains unmoved.

TRANSCENDING PRINCIPLE

There are different ways of understanding and expressing the supreme Reality. We find two definite tendencies: the tendency to stress Transcendence and the tendency to stress Immanence. A third group emerges from the combination of the two: that is Immanent Transcendence. Emphasis on Transcendence is typical of the Semitic religions: Judaism, Christianity and Islam. The emphasis on Immanence is peculiar to the Chinese religious tradition and, curiously enough, to the modern secular spirit as well. The emphasis on the Immanent aspect of Transcendence is the characteristic of the Hindu type religions, including 'tribal' religions.

Realities of the Immanent Transcendence are multi-layered and multidimensional. Man, in the ultimate sense, is not his own principle. He is related not only to his own domain but also to what is above and below him. This is illustrated by the Hindu social system, in which the Brahmana is placed at the top. The social model is derived from the cosmic model and both are hierarchical. At the transcendental level, Brahman is the supreme principle.

Man as microcosm transcends earthly limits through Cosmic intelligence and ritual action. Cosmogonic myths have revealed how the limits of the natural state were transcended in the beginning. The state of primordial solidarity was transcended as the Cosmic Egg emerged. The Earth is limited, the Sky is unlimited. Human culture is an 'Inverted Tree', with roots upward and branches downward. As the *upanishadic* sages have affirmed, 'Man as a citizen of the Earth and the Sky must make no difference'.

Man's image of the Sky is the same as of himself and of all that is here. The Sun, the Moon, the stars and the seasons are the divine manifestations, each having a name, a form and an attribute of Gods, demons, humans and animals. The ancestors of men have assumed the form of stars. The Sun and the Moon have kinship with human beings (as with Kshatriya). Man's rhythm of life is in tune with the Sky. His daily routine is organized by the cycle of the Sun; his sustenance by the cycle of the seasons; his joys (festivals) by the cycle of the Moon; and so on. Like humans, the citizens of the Sky are governed by the fourfold *varna* order. In their interpersonal relationships, like humans, they are friends, enemies and neutrals. They thrive on Man's offerings and oblations.

The correspondence between Sky and Earth is not just in appearance but in operation too. The Sky and Earth together form the cosmic rhythms of Time. Man offers sacrifice for the preservation of his own life as also of the other contingent beings. Entering into the sacrifice (the illuminant womb), Man and Time reach a state of purity and harmony — a cosmological phenomenon essential for the well-being of all. Ritual is the proper context of Man-Time interaction. It is in this context alone that Man's perception of Time can be near to what is true. For a man in tradition, properly speaking, there is no Time other than Ritual Time. There is no universal time covering all ritual events occurring everywhere through every individual. Ritual Time is not only discontinuous but also dependent on multiple Time orders. Ritual is observed at relative rest in due consideration of caste, age, sex and place.

Like Time, Space is of uneven quality; it is diverse and discontinuous. All places are not suitable for sacred performances. Some are more sacred and effective than others. Even within sacred spaces, there are purity-space and protection space. Ritual Time and Ritual Space are inextricably bound together. All bathing rituals and festivals are observed on special occasions in Ritual Space-Time.

Man, Time and Space are ritually constructed. Ritual is an aspect of *rita*, the Cosmic Law that transcends all human laws. It causes the birth and death of all corporeal beings, things and events and holds the cosmos by its own power. Whatever is created in Time (*kala*) dissolves naturally into the Great Time, *mahakala*, the God of Death. Humanly ordered Ritual Time is impermanent because ritual acts take place in an ordinal duration of Time. But all rituals are aimed at permanence, that is, transcending the impermanence of Life. There is an essential connection between Time and Great Time and Ritual Time mediates between the two.

(Ritual) Act, (Ritual) Order and (Ritual) Time are inconceivable without one another. Act is realized by the virtue of Order that occurs to create a capacity to Time. Time is not an independent reality. It is set in motion by a linear continuum of Orders within which changes occur in *kairological* moments and not in a chronological order. Hence traditional cultures give no importance to lineal history. Man's quest for return to the primordial, the ultimate goal of life, is reflected in his ritual behaviour, in the archetypal creation and dissolution of Time to experience the *kairological* moment as the rhythm of Great Time.

Change is the Law of Time. Death (Great Time) causes change; it transcends Time, but nothing transcends it. In a *cosmocentric culture,* Man transcends ordinal duration of Time in a ritual context that situates him in a state of perfect harmony with Nature and makes real his *experience* of transcendence. In a *technocentric culture,* Man ventures to transcend Time in a temporal context; and that takes him nowhere, situates him in continual strife (direct confrontation) with Nature and makes his experience unreal.

THE ONE MYSTERY

To think of anthropology is to think of the One in which all converge and from which all issue. An anthropology that studies Man in compartments and limits his self-reflective procedure is not worth pursuing. The anthropological paradigm that fails to provide a sense of *wholeness* is no good. The thoughts written in this paper have ontological foundations but they show themselves more clearly in the anthropological realm. The new paradigms suggested here have a cosmic dimension. They allow themselves to dwell within one another and reflect a deep human truth. So by virtue of logical conclusion it is named the Sacred Science of Man. It presents three original premises on which all traditional cultures stand.

Cosmic Hierophany

Brahman is the potency or principle from which all things are derived. It is the inner power and essence of all. With reference to the person, Mind is Brahman, with reference to the divinities, Space. The Brahman is identified with Brahma, the creator God and Brahmana, the human incarnation of *dharma.* The idea that Gods, humans, animals and trees are recipients of the *divine power* is not confined to India. All that is connected with this 'power concept' can, in principle, bear the name 'cosmic hierophany', where the personal and the impersonal, the animate and the inanimate, the human and the divine, the divine and the cosmic, get entirely intermingled. This aspect of the cosmic hierophany is closely bound up with the solving of the anthropologist's riddle of 'binary opposites'.

Ecological Principle

The manifested cosmoses are spatio-temporal and earthly. Man cannot live without the Earth. He is more than Earth. He is conditioned by the Law of Life. At the same time he is capable of the existential leap that takes him to another reality. The notion of the living Mother Earth and the Cosmic Cow reveals a self-perpetuating life-process grounded in the One.

Ordering Principle

The Cosmic Order sets forth the timeless sequence of creation, preservation and dissolution and plunges into the Human Order. All traditional societies are structured in terms of social formation, subsistence, distinctions and desires. Human groups are ordered by the three factors of quality which form a triadic whole. All physical and mental phenomena are held hierarchically by the permutations and combinations of the three factors. All Human Orders are subjected to the Law of Numbers (an active sacred force). Number is a cultural symbol that plays a unique and privileged role in determining the hierarchy of infinite sets which are incomprehensible or else chaotic. It is an aspect of cosmodicy, *rita*. The *Rita* is a class of non-equilibrium systems that self-organize. It stands for both chaos and order, interior and exterior, separation and union, forming a great complexus keeping the flow of Time.

Bibliography

Agrawala, Vasudeva S. 1963. *Matsya Purana: A Study*. Varanasi: All India Kashiraj Trust.

Butt, Gary and Frena Bloomfield. 1985. *Harmony Rules*. London: Arrow Books.

Davies, Paul and John Gribbin. 1992. *The Matter Myth: Beyond Chaos and Complexity*. London: Penguin Books.

Gonda, J. 1950. *Notes on Brahman*. Utrecht: J.L. Beyers.

Hume, Robert Ernest. 1984. *The Thirteen Principal Upanishads: Translated from the Sanskrit*. New Delhi: Oxford University Press.

Lalye, P.G. 1995. 'The Panca Mahabhutas'. In *Prakriti: The Integral Vision*. Vol. 4. (ed.) Jayant V. Narlikar. New Delhi: IGNCA & D.K. Printworld.

Lawlor, Robert. 1991. *Voices of the First Day: Awakening in the Aboriginal Dream Time*. Rochester: Inner Traditions International.

Malville, J.M. 1997. 'The Cosmic Geometries of Vijayanagar'. In *Ancient Cities, Sacred Skies: Cosmic Geometries and City Planning in Ancient India*. New Delhi: IGNCA & Aryan Books International.

Morries, Henry M. 1974. *Scientific Creationism*. San Diego: Creation Life Publishers.

Panikkar, Raimundo. 1976. 'Time and History in the Tradition of India: *Kala* and *Karma'* (with an appendix by Bettina Baumer, on the empirical apperception of time). In *Cultures and Time*. Paris: The Unesco Press.

——. 1977. *The Vedic Experience: Mantramanjari: An Anthology of the Vedas for Modern Man and Contemporary Celebration*. London: Darton, Longman and Todd.

——. 1993. *The Cosmotheandric Experience: Emerging Religious Consciousness*. New York: Orbis Books.

Prasad, Onkar 1999. 'Sound as Harmony: A Case of the Acoustic Environment of Santhals'. In *Dhavani: Nature and Culture of Sound*. (ed.) S.C. Malik. New Delhi: IGNCA & D.K. Printworld.

Sabarathinam, S.P. 1995. 'Agamic Treatment of Mahabhutas in Relation to Mandalas and Arts'. In *Prakrite: The Integral Vision*. Vol. 3. (ed.) Bettina Baumer. New Delhi: IGNCA & D.K. Printworld.

Sarakar, Bharati. 1999. 'Communication Through Sound in Animals'. In *Dhavani: Nature and Culture of Sound*. (ed.) S.C. Malik. New Delhi: IGNCA & D.K. Printworld.

Saran, A.K. 1996. *Traditional Thought: Toward an Axiomatic Approach*. Sarnath, Varanasi: Central Institute of Higher Tibetan Studies.

Saraswati, Baidyanath. 1991. 'Ritual Space: Tribal Nontribal Context'. In *Concepts of Space: Ancient and Modern*. (ed.) Kapila Vatsyayan. New Delhi: IGNCA.

——. 1994. 'Animal Ontology: The Hindu Vision of Tradition'. In *Conference on Animal: A Reappraisal*. Toronto: Victoria University.

——. 1995. 'Cosmogonic Myths in North-East India: Forces of Nature'. In *Prakriti: The Integral Vision*. Vol. 1. (ed.) Baidyanath Saraswati. New Delhi: IGNCA & D.K. Printword.

——. 1995. 'Forms of Life in the World of Matter: Reflections on Tribal Cosmology'. In *Prakriti: The Integral Vision*, Vol. 4. (ed.) J.V. Narlikar. New Delhi: IGNCA & D.K. Printworld.

——. 1995. 'Elements of Nature and the Order of Culture'. In *Prakriti: The Integral Vision*. Vol. 5. (ed.) Baidyanath Saraswati. New Delhi: IGNCA & D.K. Printworld.

——. 1995. 'The Living Universe: A Unitary Vision'. In *Universal Responsibility: A Felicitation Volume in Honour of His Holiness the Fourteenth Dalai Lama, Tenzin Gyatso, on His Sixtieth Birthday*. (eds.) Ramesh Chandra Tiwari and Krishna Nath. New Delhi: ANB Publishers.

——. 1995. *The Sacred Science of Nature: The Verrier Elwin Memorial Lectures*. Shillong: North-Eastern Hill University.

——. 1996. 'Ritual Time: An Exegesis of Time and Great Time'. In *Concept of Time: Ancient and Modern*. (ed.) Kapila Vatsyayan. New Delhi: IGNCA.

——. 1999. 'Echoes of the Cosmic Play'. In *Cosmology of the Sacred World: The Vision of the Cosmos of Different Peoples of the World*. (eds.) Baidyanath Saraswati and Yolott Gonzalez Torres. New Delhi: Decent Books.

——. 1999. 'Thinking About Sound in Traditional Sciences'. In *Dhvani: Nature and Culture of Sound*. (ed.) S.C. Malik, New Delhi: IGNCA & D.K. Printworld.

——. 2001. 'Alternative Paradigms in Anthropology: The Cosmic Anthropological Principle'. In *The Nature of Man and Culture*. (ed.) Baidyanath Saraswati. New Delhi: IGNCA & Aryan Books International.

——. 2001. 'Mind the Elephant: A Sacred Science View of Reality'. In *Mind, Man and Mask (Rupa-Pratirupa)*. (ed.) S.C. Malik. New Delhi: IGNCA & Aryan Books International.

——. 2001. 'Nature as Culture: The Vision of Tradition'. In *Santhal World-view*. (ed.) Nita Mathur. New Delhi: IGNCA & Concept Publishing Company.

——. 2001. 'Parampara: A Universal Paradigm'. In *The Nature of Living Tradition—Distinctive Features of Indian Parampara*. (ed.) Baidyanath Saraswati. New Delhi: IGNCA & D.K. Printworld.

Sharma, Prem Lata. 1995. 'Mahabhutas in Sangita-Sastra: With Special Reference to Yoga and Ayurveda'. In *Prakriti: The Integral Vision*. Vol. 3. (ed.) Bettina Baumer. New Delhi: IGNCA & D.K. Printworld.

Vatsyayan, Kapila. 1993. *Indian Art: The One and the Many — The Jawaharlal Nehru Memorial Lectures*. London: The Nehru Centre.

Williams, Robert Charles. 1983. 'Scientific Creationism: An Exegesis of a Religious Doctrine'. In *American Anthropologist,* No. 85.

Yogananda, Paramhansa. 1995. *The Bhagavad Gita*, Chaps 1-5. California: Self-Realization Fellowship.

Index

Abhidharmakosha 54
African societies 48
Agamas 31
Air (element) 2, 20, 21, 23, 24, 25, 26, 29, 31, 32, 33, 34, 36, 40, 41, 65, 103, 116
Airavat (celestial elephant) 11, 96
Algerian peasants 48
Anahatnada 49
Ananta (thousand-headed gigantic serpent) 11, 12
Anaximander 71, 72
Animal
  vehicles of Gods 11
  weirdness 14, 15
Anthropic principle 55
Apa Tani's eschatological belief 69
Arjuna 56
Artificial intelligence 1
Aruni 6, 53
Astrology 14, 17, 77, 107, 115
Atharvaveda 40, 73, 91
Atman (self, soul) 17, 21, 49, 51, 52, 53, 92, 93
Australian aboriginal myth 40, 42, 44, 45
Autotelic science 1, 109, 119
Ayurveda 24, 28, 29

Beyond inner and outer 35, 70
Bhagavata Purana 54
Bhagvad Gita 56
Bharatnatyam 36
Bhavaputra 96
Big Bang 4, 7, 44
Biological clock (time) 48, 72, 79, 81, 87
Bodhisattva 11
Body of the Universe 13, 51, 56
Bonga, a Munda term 115
Brahma (God of creature) 8
  See also Expanding universe, Mind, Sound, Soundless 2, 4, 7, 8, 9, 11, 12, 19, 32, 53, 58, 59, 62, 75, 86, 115, 121
Brahma Purana 59
Brahman 3, 4, 5, 6, 7, 12, 21, 35, 37, 38, 39, 44, 46, 47, 51, 54, 56, 62, 67, 68, 73, 74, 81, 92, 95, 102
Brahmana 59, 60, 61, 82, 105, 115, 118, 119, 121
Brihadaranyaka Upanisada 5, 6, 28, 39, 52, 53, 92
Buddha 11, 17, 58, 59, 72, 117

Cambrian 9
Cannibalism 14
Chandogya Upanisada 39, 52, 92
Charles Darwin 106
Christian
  theology 105
  traid 19
Christianity 69, 119
Composite forms, anthropomorphic and zoomorphic 11
Cosmic
  anthropological principle 101
  egg 9, 19, 20, 102, 103, 106, 119

fish 9
hierophany 116, 121, 122
intelligence 3, 16, 109, 112, 119
law 62, 88, 106, 120
law of return 105
order 24, 88, 92, 118, 122
person 6, 20, 51, 64, 77, 111
play 62, 64, 66, 67, 95
sound 4, 7, 40
time 62, 72, 77
time-person 77
Cosmocentric culture 110, 121
Cosmology
ocean 10, 106
pauranic 53, 54
time 74, 75
tribal 24
upanisadic 22
vedic 20, 22, 53
Cow
measure of ontological change 17
wish-fulfilling 10, 66, 116
Creation- *See* Creation two kinds:: Creation, substitute creation,
Creation age (yuga) 7
Creation-sound 44
Creation two kinds:- *See* Creation two kinds: natural, unnatural
Culture
anthropocentric 110
cosmocentric 110, 121
fourfold 110
technocentric 110, 121
theocentric 110

Darwinian conception
evolution 111
nature 111
Deluge 8
Dependent origination 72, 117
Descartes, Rene 100, 106
Devonian 9
Dharmashastra 101
Dogon of Africa 40
Dragon's head and tail 14, 77

Earth (element) 2, 40
Ecological principle 116, 122
Einstein's theory of relativity 82
Element 2, 6, 20, 21, 22, 23, 24, 25, 26, 27, 28, 29, 30, 31, 32, 33, 34, 35, 40, 41, 45, 51, 83, 84, 102, 103, 110, 111, 116, 117, 118
Endless space 53
Eschatology 107
Euclidean geometry 19
Evolutionist 103
Expanding Universe 4, 44, 97
Experiencing time 80
Expert system 1

Fire (element) 6, 11, 21
First threes 62
Five primordial elements 103, 118
Five sheaths (*kosa*) 21
Four castes of men 6, 20, 60
Four stages of life 105

Gai, Greek Goddess of Earth 6
Gajanan 96
Ganapati hypothesis 97, 99
Gandharva 2, 33
Ganga 11, 59, 82, 83, 88, 118
Garbha Upanisada 23
Gargi 1, 2, 3
Geometrical forms 36
Geometry of God 7
Gigibori, a Suau-Tawala (Papua) term 116
God with infinite forms 11
Godavari 59
Golden Germ 1, 3, 20, 22, 51, 53, 54, 102
Great soul 51
Great time 72, 75, 81, 83, 85, 86, 87, 88, 89, 90, 120, 121

Greek goddess 6
Greeks 50, 72

Heaven 3, 8, 11, 16, 53, 56, 62, 66
Hindu
  antithetical of creationism 106
  pantheon 10, 106
Hinduism 69
Homo sapiens 117
Human beings, four categories 105
Human desires, four categories 105

Immanent transcendence 119
Incarnation, three kinds 8
Indian music 49
Indra, the king of Gods 2, 7
Infinite void 63
Inner controller 6, 28, 53, 54, 92, 98, 107, 116
Inverted flute 87, 109
Isa Upanisada 73
Islam 69, 119

Jackal 12, 42, 43, 113
Jain places of pilgrimage 58
Jambudvipa 54, 55
Jangam tirthas 59
Jharkhand 61
Jim Lovelock 6
Judaism 119
Jupiter 55, 66, 115

Kabir 87, 94, 109
Kairological moment 84, 85, 89, 121
Kalapurusa 77
Kalatirtha 79
Kashi-ksetra 60, 67, 88
Katha Upanisada 15, 39, 74, 92
Kathak 36
Kathakali 36
Kaushitaki Upanisada 91, 99
Khasis 69, 70
Kinetic order 86
Krishna, the universal spirit 17, 96
Krishna's flute 43
Krsnadvaipayana Vyasa 96
Ksetra 57, 58
Kshatriya 81, 82, 105, 115, 118, 120
Kumbha 66, 80

Life-breath 107
Life-principle 51, 53, 62
Life-sap 9
Lord of planetary directions 77, 83
Lord of quarters 14
Lovelock, Jim 6
Luminous space 62

Mahabharata 58, 96
Mahadaniya villages 61
Mahakala, the Great Time 72, 75, 83, 87, 88, 89, 120
Mahasmasana 63
Mahavedi 36
Mahayuga 7, 8
Mahesha, God of death and dissolution 7, 8
Maitri Upanisada 38, 74, 94
Man and mind 94, 95
Mana, a Polynesian term for power 116
Manastirthas 59
Manava Dharmashastra 101
Mandala 53, 54, 58, 62
Manipuri 36
Manu-principle 101, 104
Mask 95, 96, 97, 98, 99
Matter and life 44, 91, 92
Maya 56, 94, 95, 99
Mezatec Indians of New Mexico 47
Milky Way 5, 53
Mind 5, 6, 15, 20, 46, 57, 91, 92, 93
  and Body 92, 111
  as Brahman 98
  as cosmos and chaos 108

Mind-born son 96
Minkowski's theory 83
Mithi (Mithil, Mithila) 77, 85
Mokshatirtha 59
Moon 2
Mount Sumeru 54
Multiple time systems 81
Music of spheres 50

Nadabindu 44, 45
Nadabrahman 44, 49
Naksatrapurusa 77
Nannool 35
Nature
  elements of 22, 23, 111
  laws of 43
  Newtonian view 111
  three qualities 13, 17
Natyasastra 34, 49
Nawalak, a Kwakiutl term for Brahman 115
Newton, Isaac 4, 79
Nine planets 20

Om, primary sound 35, 38, 39, 41, 49
Onge 19
Ontological change 17, 107
Oraon 61
Ordering principle 118, 122
Ornithologists 41

Paniniya Siksa 33
Pauranic
  anthropology 96
  cosmology 53, 54
Permenides 72
Pisces 115
Pitha 46, 58
Planets, attributes of 76
Prajapati 2
Prasna Upanisada 91, 92
Prajapati, the father of creatures 2, 8, 91, 104
Purusa (Cosmic Person) 6, 20, 21, 23, 51, 64, 66, 77, 97, 102
Pythagoras 50

Quadrangle symbolizes the cosmic time 62
Quantum physics 5
  uncertainty principle 48
Question of question (atiprasna) 3

Ragas 49
Ramayana 14, 61
Revelation 54
Rigveda 3, 4, 16, 19, 21, 47, 70, 92, 94, 104, 116, 118
Ritual
  language 112, 113
  space 61, 69, 82, 83, 84, 89, 120
  time 77, 79, 80, 81, 82, 84, 85, 87, 89, 120

Sabari Malai hills 68
Sabdabrahman 39, 44, 45, 47
Sacred
  numbers 19
  space 56, 57, 61, 68, 88
Samveda 19, 53, 62
Sanctum sanctorum 61, 69
Sangitapurusa 49
Saraswati, the Goddess 11, 47
Satapatha Brahmana 91
Scientific creationism 103
Scorpio 115
Self-organizing system 3
Semitic tradition 4
Seven great ones 20, 54
Shaft of light (*jyotirlinga*) 59
Shaman (diviner) 47
Shankaracharya 58, 82
Shihlu (Chinese character) 48
Shilpasastra 36

Shiva 11, 12, 15, 20, 31, 32, 34, 35, 45, 46, 58, 62, 63, 65, 72, 88, 96, 97
both male and female 11
eight-footed 12
five-faced 20
half-Vishnu and half-Shiva 11
pashupati 11
Shakti 31
three eyes 12
Shudra 60, 82, 115, 118
Shukracharya 66
Siddhanta Jyotis 82
Silurian 9
Skanda Purana 66
Sky (element) 26, 33, 40
Sound
brahman 49
causal 20, 33
chaotic 44
Chinese concept 44
cosmic 4, 7
musical 33, 34
particle 35
particles 35, 45
space 35
Sufi tradition 49
Soundless Brahman 38, 49
Space 21, 25, 45, 51, 52, 53, 56, 60, 61, 82, 88, 89, 101, 104, 111, 115, 120, 121
-time 82, 83, 84, 88, 89, 98, 110, 114
inner 35, 36, 49, 50
outer 35, 45
protection 61, 82, 120
ritual 69, 82, 83, 84, 89, 120
sacred 56, 57
time 120
Sphota 46
Sruti (revealed text) 21, 49
Stars 2
Sthavara tirthas 59
Sun 2
Svetasvatara Upanisada 74
Swastika of Brahma 53
Symbiosis 15, 16, 107
Tittiriya Upanisada 21, 51, 92, 94
Tandava (dance) 45
Tantric ritual 46
Taurus 115
Theodicy as cosmodicy 105, 108
Tianshi (heavenly time) 75
Time 28, 48, 71, 72, 73, 77
-measure 45
biological 48, 72, 79, 81
biology 15
cosmological 7
experiencing 80
heavenly 75
person 14, 77, 78
ritual 77, 79, 81, 82, 84, 85, 86, 88, 89, 120
worship 84
Tirtha 59, 60
-ksetra 57, 58
Tirthankara 59
Totem 107
Tradition as Hiero-history 113
Transcendence of time 85
Transforming principle 67

Ultimate reality 38, 93, 108, 109
Unification principle 114
Universal 13, 17, 19, 20, 24, 50, 57, 62, 79, 81, 93, 97, 98, 101, 116
Universe
as living animal 1
borrowed from vacuum 5
expanding 4
of brahman 56, 62, 95
of multiplicity 4, 102
self-designed 106
Upanisadic cosmology 22

Vaisesika system of philosophy 26

Vaishya 60, 81, 82, 115, 118
Varna 46, 60, 75, 103, 105, 115, 120
Vastusastra 36
Vedanga Jyotisa 82
Vedic cosmology 20
  prajapati 77
  revelation 46, 52
  sage 21, 72
Venus 55, 115
Vikrama samvata 78
Vishnu 7, 8, 9, 10, 11, 12, 15, 17, 32, 46, 53, 55, 58, 66, 80, 86, 106
Vishwarupa (gd of majesty with infinite forms) 11

Wakan, a Siouan term for Brahaman 115
Water (element) 2, 21, 29
Word as World 108
Word of
  man 15
  Manu 101
  Indra 2
  stars 2
  phenomena 1
  snake 15
Word-principle (three states) 108
World of
  cow 14
  god 15, 108

Xiaosheng, a Chinese term for human sound, laughter 44

Yajnavalkya 1, 3, 6
Yajurveda 19, 53, 62
Yamuna 11, 83
Yang and *yin* (Chinese term) 30, 31, 43, 44
yuga, a creation age 7

Zero
  brahman 3, 4, 97
  fullness 19
  sunya 4, 38, 102
  ultimate 38
Zodiac 46, 71, 77, 78, 79, 80, 115